How Shall We Then Forgive

Jeff Quill

ISBN 978-1477429853

To Aunt Kay
Who Loved Me

ACKNOWLEDGMENTS

Thank you Lord for my friends and family who showed love,
patience and skill in helping me through this work. Gayle Quill,
Terry and Janet Biggart, Hazel Torgimson, Bob Langan,
Ellen Langan, Neil Schindler, Paul Baker, Larry Fayhe.
I love you all.

Contents

Jeff Quill

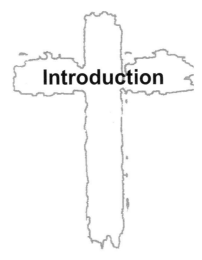

Introduction

Let my people go. Exodus 5:1

"How can I possibly forgive?" asked a young friend of mine who was devastated by her husband's infidelity. In earlier discussions, she heatedly asserted that Christianity was the cause of most, if not all of the world's problems. I understood her position. But hoping she could rise above it, I told her as gently as I could, how a Christian forgives.

"You can't tell me that," she blurted angrily.

I replied, "It's who I am. It's all I have to offer you. It's the only way I know."

She composed herself, "Yes." And her voice trailed off, "Yes, of course."

As for secular methods of forgiveness, I had none I could confidently suggest. I wish I did. As of this writing she continues to suffer from the wound, and worse, picks at it daily. But God wants something better for us all, and God has something better for us all.

This book is about a distinctively Christian forgiveness. By forgiving in the way described here, a non-Christian will become Christian. I recommend that. Christ is the deepest desire of all persons. He is forever their most radical thirst, and at the same time, the perfect quenching of that thirst. He is the sweetness that overwhelms all bitterness, and the peace that quiets all turmoil. If, dear reader, you are a non-believer, read on. You may wander into joy, meeting the Christ: the Truth Who makes us free.[1]

Let Birds Fly...Genesis 1:20

According to scripture, *the heavens are telling us about the glory of God,*[2] and according to astronomers, those heavens are ever expanding. This means that the stars show us God's un-bounded hugeness and wide-open nature. God is forever expansive, unlimited, and free. As the poet says,

Open up, open up, God is ever open up.

This unbounded nature is why He found the shackles on His people Israel so intolerable. He commanded the world's most powerful ruler, "*Let my people go.*" In all these millennia since, nothing has changed. He looks at the bitterness and animosity enslaving His children and says, "Let my people go. Let them forgive. Let them *soar on wings like eagles*, break the gravity of resentment, and live free." His passion for our freedom drove Him to the extreme measures of that first "Good Friday," and His quest for our liberation takes Him from broad and bright high-Heaven down to the dark, bolted cellars of our souls.

How To Get The Most Out Of This Book

While you can read this book at whatever pace is good for you, I recommend that you don't hurry. Read just one chapter a day. It is set up for that. The chapters are short so that you may read them again if need be. If something touches you, set the book aside, and contemplate that. Let God work His truth in your heart.

The Bible is used extensively within these pages so you may have confidence that what is presented is based on the Word of God. God plants a trust of Holy Writ deep in the hearts of His children.[3] "*Let the word of Christ dwell in you richly,*"[4] building your faith. If a question arises as you read, jot it down and set it aside. Your question may be answered in a later chapter.

I shared an early manuscript of this book with a few people. A couple of them, who were fully convinced they could never forgive, avoided reading it. One did not start, and the other drew back and stalled midway through. If you are absolutely sure you cannot forgive, know that the Nazarene, who loved you more than

His own life, is absolutely sure that you **can** forgive. In deference to His opinion, please, read through. You will be glad you did. May your heart alight upon the treasure within these pages.

1John 8:31; 2Psalm 19:1; 3John 10:4,5,27;4Colossians 3:16

Note About Quotes:

Quotes are taken from the King James Version, usually with light modernization (i.e. updating thee, thou, thy, hath, doth, and etcetareth.) What is not from the Authorized Version is the author's rendering, condensation, or compilation. Bible quotes are *italicized*. Chapter and verse references are listed at the end of each chapter. The names in my stories have been changed to insure anonymity and to guard privacy.

Jeff Quill

Chapter One

An Invitation

The little barefoot boy stood in the kitchen looking at his mother's bloody face as she swayed back and forth. His father, huffing and wobbling in drunken rage, roared at her, "See what you made me do? Are you happy now?"

Then turning to the children standing in line with the boy, "Are you happy now?" None of the four spoke. His eyes burned wide and he hissed deeply "Are – You – Happ – Eeee – Naaaa – Oww."

"Yes Daddy," cried Patty, the eldest.

The drunk glared at Mark, the next in line. "Yes sir," he whimpered in a voice that was ready to duck.

To Mark's right Kevin answered almost in unison, but pleadingly louder. The three-year-old boy, however, stood silent in shocked bewilderment. The man set his stare on the child, but the boy could see nothing but his tortured mother trying to stay on her feet. Kevin knew the danger coming at the little one, and as if to wake him up, he gently shook the child's shoulder calling his name. The barefoot boy looked at the terror stricken face of his older brother.

"Are you happy?" asked Kevin. Happy? Never before had the boy heard the word "Happy". This hot, swelling throb in his head and chest that made it hard to breathe must be "Happy."

1

"Yes," he confessed. "I'm happy." He turned back to his mother only to see his father's fist connect with her cheek. Her feet shot forward, her head jerked back and a grunt of air burst from her chest as she hit linoleum with a loud thud.

"Mommy!" screamed the boy. He broke line and ran toward his mother. His body moved too slowly for his panicked heart. Reaching the woman. He grabbed her hand.

"Get up mommy, get up." he begged with a tear soaked face.

"Mommy's OK, Honey," she smiled. "Get back in line... please."

With that interruption, the drunken man staggered from the room. The children, with the softest step they could manage, hurried themselves and the little boy up the creaking stairs to hide in their beds, afraid to whisper or to sleep. They had seen this before.

Given what this family went through, given what this boy went through, how shall he then forgive? As I am that little barefoot boy, how shall I then forgive?

One night, decades after this memory, after my own children had grown and moved away, I could not get to sleep. At four a.m., I was still pacing. Indignation smoldered in my head, fueled by some nasty church politics. My pride stinging and my stomach knotted, I fumed over the injustice. Eventually, I came to the end of myself. I then asked God to help me let go of my anger. He showed me how to forgive and then walked me through it.

The next emotion keeping me awake was joy. Elated, I danced through the house, laughing and singing. The torment ceased, and a weight, which I had no idea was there, lifted. Over the next few weeks and days I eagerly tried to remember old hurts just so I could forgive them. This joy, this freedom of forgiving, is what I want to share with you.

Good News

Christian, we can forgive. If ever you battled the soul-rooted weed of bitterness, then you know that this is actually amazing news. God has a bountiful gift for us: a forgiving heart; a loving, free, and joyous heart. Let's look for it. As we do we shall find a soothing balm for old wounds and a miraculous antidote to poisonous memories.

Don't be afraid of this. Jesus said, *"Fear not little flock. It is the Father's good pleasure to give you the kingdom."*1 This ability to forgive, like everything else in God's kingdom, is given to us freely by our loving Heavenly Father. The apostle Paul tells us what the kingdom looks like: *"The kingdom of God is... righteousness, and peace, and joy in the Holy Ghost."*2 It is God's great delight to give us the righteousness known as forgiveness so that peace and joy may flood our lives.

We were made for this. Picture God as a master toolmaker. We walk into his shop and see the shelves lined with people.

"What are these?" we ask.

"Aren't they beautiful?" He beams.

"Why, yes," we answer, "But what do they do?"

"They forgive." boasts the toolmaker. "Completely and without reservation. Amazing, eh?" God created us for good things, like forgiving.

*For we are His workmanship, created in Christ Jesus for good works, which God has beforehand prepared for us to walk in them.*3

According to this verse we are made to do things that are already done: the forgiveness is already there. Now picture God as a master builder, building a house for us. From foundation to weather vane, the only material He used is love. It is already ours, just waiting for us to take possession. We need only walk in and own it. These works were prepared before we came along so that we can reside in them now. God Himself will move us into the house of forgiveness.

The Will

I had a pastor who asked, "Do you want to want to forgive?"4 And you, dear reader, the fact that you are reading this book is proof that you want to forgive. It is evidence of the forgiveness of God already stirring in your heart. God is helping you right now, *working in you to will and to do of His good pleasure.*5 You may struggle with forgiveness, but you **are** struggling. If there was no forgiveness in your heart, you would not concern yourself. Because we are willing to let God work in us, we shall be healed. He will show us how to forgive....

1Luke 12:32; 2Romans14:17; 3Ephesians 2:10; 4Rev. Dennis Bennet; 5Philippians 2:13

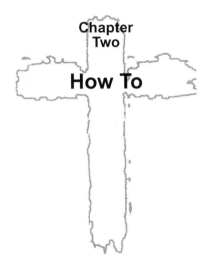

Chapter Two

How To

A world-famous religious leader came to our town. The local news covered his visit almost hour by hour. Devout throngs cherished his every word. The highlight of his week was a segment aired on local programs for days. He told the multitude what forgiveness looked like. The description was sound. He said, "Though I remember what you did, I still have concern for you."

A mighty cheer arose from the adoring crowd. "Wonderful." I thought, "But how does that happen?" To that, no answer came. Regardless of the thrill running through the faithful, hearing a virtue described is not possession of it. I was un-enthused.

Our Search

Tormented souls seeking a way to forgive spend fortunes renting the psychiatrist's couch, with little effect. Caring counselors offer rituals and exercises that hardly ease the harsh misery of resentment. Our doctors lecture us on the health risk of grudges. Our clergy sermonize on the spiritual consequence of rancor, exhorting us to completely, quickly, and constantly forgive. Though repeatedly assured of the benefits in "letting go," and warned of the fallout in "holding on," are we shown how to forgive? Barely and rarely and really not at all. We know something of **what** for-

5

giveness is, and **when** it ought to happen. We know **where** it applies, and **who** should get it. We know who is obliged to employ it. But **how** do we forgive? **How? How? How?** How does this *stony heart become a soft heart of flesh*?₁ How does bitter become sweet, and *the leopard lose his spots*?₂ How can we change?

It is not that we don't want to forgive; rather it appears that we **can't.** It seems like we could walk on water and turn it into wine before turning our inner vinegar to honey. We feel we do not forgive, because we feel we **cannot** forgive. From the Psalms: *"The law of the LORD is perfect, restoring the soul."*₃ As we look into His Word, He will restore our peace, and make the changes we need.

Better

Our hearts are meant for better things. Things that accompany salvation, like love, serenity, and a quiet conscience. The God who asks us to forgive will show us how and enable us to do so. From the Holy Scriptures He will give His counsel. It works. By the Holy Spirit He will endow us with His love. For the believer in Jesus Christ, it is the solution.

I heard a woman say, as she tried to solve a party game puzzle, "If you understand, it's awfully simple. If you don't, it's simply awful." David continues his song, *"the testimony of the LORD is sure, making wise the simple."*₃ Our Father's Word clears up confusion and breaks down the complex for all those who, like me, are simple.

The Coming Pages

In the coming pages we will examine how to forgive. We will look at the basis of forgiveness and the scriptural foundation for absolution of wrongs done to us. We will identify the roadblocks: those things that keep us from our goal. We will explore the ways we can move on – the ways we **shall** move on. This will all build on itself, preparing our hearts. Chapter by chapter, *precept upon precept, line upon line, line upon line, here a little, and there a little*₄ God will uncover forgiveness and peace for us. Let's take our time and allow Him to reveal His mercy in our depths. He has a way for us. He will lead us to it and through it.

It Is Finished

We begin at the end. As Jesus died He cried out, *"It is finished."*5 It was the hardest thing He ever said, because He went through hell to say it. This victory cry from the darkest moment in history, rings deep in believing hearts. As we search God's word for His marvelous gift, these three words will be a breath prayer to hold us until we come upon that *treasure hidden in earthen vessels.*6 We say with Christ, "It is finished." Pray to our Father, "It is finished." For now, we whisper to our hearts "It is finished." To unforgiveness and the unforgiven declare, "It is finished."

One may ask, "How can we say, 'It is finished', when clearly, it is not." Let our Lord handle that. "It is finished," is the prayer of Him *who calls those things that be not as though they were, those future things as though they were past.*7 It is the prayer of Him who already sees us forgiving like He wants us to. And as we shall see, at its heart, forgiveness is prayer. From His cross He says, "It is finished". We bow our hearts in agreement before the crucified Christ, saying with Him from the start, "It is finished."

Let's start now by looking at what **not** to try...

1Ezeliel 11:19; 2Jeremiah 13:23; 3Psalm 19:7; 4 Isaih 28:10; 5John 19:30; 62Cor 4:7; 7Romans 4:17

Jeff Quill

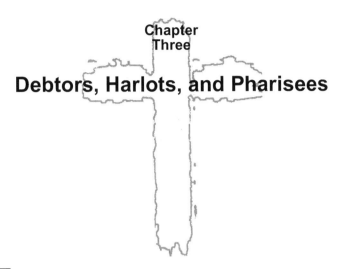

Chapter Three

Debtors, Harlots, and Pharisees

*T*herefore, the kingdom of heaven is like a king who wanted to settle accounts with his servants. As he began the settlement, a man who owed him ten thousand talents was brought to him. Since he was not able to pay, the master ordered that he and his wife and his children and all that he had be sold to repay the debt. The servant fell on his knees before him.

"Be patient with me," he begged, "and I will pay back everything."

The servant's master took pity on him, canceled the debt, and let him go. But when that servant went out, he found one of his fellow servants who owed him a hundred denarii. He grabbed him and began to choke him.

"Pay back what you owe me!" he demanded. His fellow servant fell to his knees and begged him, "Be patient with me, and I will pay you back." But he refused. Instead, he went off and had the man thrown into prison until he could pay the debt. When the other servants saw what had happened, they were greatly distressed and went and told their master everything that had happened. Then the master called the servant in.

"You wicked servant," he said, "I canceled all that debt of yours because you begged me to. Shouldn't you have had mercy on your fellow servant just as I had on you?" In anger his master

---

*turned him over to the jailers to be tortured, until he should pay back all he owed.*₁

Wrong Way

This teaching from our Lord about forgiveness is not a success story. This is an illustration of what not to do. Instead of showing us a model of someone able to forgive, someone following the king's example, The Lord shows us a complete failure. The narrative challenges our assumptions about how to forgive.

The Lord does not want us to get the idea that this is something we can do any better than the *wicked servant*. Hans Christian Anderson tells a tale of a Prince who says, "Oh, why did Eve take of the tree of knowledge? Why did Adam eat the forbidden fruit? If it had only been I, it would never have happened. And sin would never have entered the world."

He finds his way back to Eden only to fail worse than Adam. We are mistaken in presuming success where others failed, even knowing the story ahead of time. Like the fellow servants in the Lord's parable, we look on in horror at the bully's actions. Paul confronts our uneasiness, *"You have no excuse because…You who judge do the same things."*₂

A man forgiven hundreds of thousands of dollars throws a fellow servant into debtors prison for pennies. What went wrong here? What should have happened did not happen. Freed of so much, why was he unable to forgive such a tiny debt? It was because he did not take to heart the mercy of the king. His were not the actions of a forgiven man. He behaved like a nasty character still trying to raise money to cover a debt. Blind to the kindness of the throne, he went after his fellow servant and the paltry debt. Maybe he did not understand that the pardon was not free; covering the debt cost his king dearly. If he did consider that point, he thought little of it.

The Harlot

In another story of a compassionate King we see a different response from the debtor.

One of the Pharisees invited Him to dinner. And He went into the Pharisee's house, and sat down to eat, and, behold, a woman in the city, who was a sinner, heard that Jesus dined in the Pharisee's house, brought an alabaster box of ointment, and

10

stood at His feet behind Him weeping, and began to wash His feet with tears, and wipe them with the hairs of her head, kissed His feet, and anointed them with the ointment.

Now when the Pharisee who had invited Him saw this, he thought to himself, "This man, if He were a prophet, would have known who and what manner of woman this is that touches him: for she is a sinner."

Jesus said to him, "Simon, I have something to say to you."

And he said, "Master, say on."

"There was a certain creditor who had two debtors: the one owed five hundred dollars, and the other fifty. And when they had nothing to pay, he frankly forgave them both. Tell Me therefore, which of them will love him most?"

Simon answered, "I suppose that he, to whom he forgave most."

And He said to him, "You have rightly judged." And He turned to the woman, and said to Simon, "Do you see this woman? I entered your house, you gave Me no water for My feet: but she has washed My feet with tears, and wiped them with the hair of her head. You gave Me no kiss: but this woman, since the time I came in has not ceased to kiss My feet. You did not anoint My head with oil: but this woman has anointed My feet with ointment. And so, to You I say, her sins, which are many, are forgiven; thus, she loves much: but to whom little is forgiven, the same loves but a little."

*And He said unto her, "Your sins are forgiven."*3

Jesus says here, "You can tell that this woman was forgiven much, because she loves so much." He was not saying that she was forgiven because she loved. That would mean she earned the grace of God. No one earns or deserves God's grace. Rather, He was saying that she loved because she was freely given something she did not and could not merit. He assures her of what she already knows deep in her heart. *"Your sins are forgiven."*

The person, who thinks his transgression is no great thing to forgive, will love little. To whom little is forgiven, the same loves little. To whom much is forgiven, the same loves much. Does that mean if I really love God I commit bigger sins for Him to forgive?4

That is obviously silly. The smallest nibble of sin is big enough to damn any soul. Consider Eve.5

My devotion to my Lord reflects how I see my debt – how much I think He forgave. To me, it is a lot to forgive. In my view, much is forgiven. In my estimation, much is pardoned. The more I understand what He forgave me, the more I love my God. Let me therefore see more...

1Matthew 18:23-34; 2Romans 2:1; 3Luke 7:36-50; 4Romans 3:8; 5Genesis 3:6

Chapter Four

The Good Man

In the story of the wicked servant we saw contempt for mercy; consider now the attitude of another servant: John the Baptist. He was the consummate **good man**. Here is an angel's testimony about him: *"He shall be great in the sight of the Lord, and shall drink neither wine nor strong drink; and he shall be filled with the Holy Ghost, even from his mother's womb. And many of the children of Israel shall he turn to the Lord their God."*[1] Arrow-straight from infancy on, he inspired devotion to God wherever he went.

Here is Jesus' testimony of him: *"Verily I say unto you, among them that are born of women there has not arisen a greater than John the Baptist."*[2] In the Lord's opinion, this man was the cream topping the milk bottle. Even his detractors questioned whether he was the prophet Elijah or even the Christ.[3]

Now look at John's testimony of himself: *"I am just a voice in the desert, but after me there comes one so much greater that I am not worthy to stoop down and untie His shoes."*[4] Unlike the gentlewoman in the house of Simon, John, who Jesus thought was one of the finest men to ever live, would not presume to remove the Lord's shoes, let alone wash His feet. Why? His reverence was due to His appreciation of God's forgiveness. His father Zacharias prophesied that John would share *the knowledge of*

13

salvation with his people by the forgiveness of their sins, through the tender mercy of our God.[5] John loved the tender mercy of God, and understood forgiveness. To him, it was everything. To this very righteous, Spirit-filled man, much was forgiven – therefore he loved much. In this man we can see that the more we appreciate God's kindness toward us, the stronger we tie into the source of forgiveness.

The trouble with the wicked servant was that to him, little was forgiven – therefore he loved little. Because he closed his heart to the king's compassion, he could not open it to others; setting aside the king's kindness, he had none to offer. He laid hold of his colleague's throat, because he did not lay hold of forgiveness. We see no evidence of love for his king. Since a love for God fuels forgiveness, a lukewarm devotion yields a tepid mercy.

John, in bold contrast, burns with adoration. He said that he *rejoiced greatly* just to hear the voice of Jesus; that it made his *joy complete.*[6] The thankfully forgiven rejoice in the shining face of absolute love.

Merry ol' souls

Merry are they whose wrong doings are forgiven, whose sins are covered. Joyful is the man whose sin the Lord will never hold against him.[7] God's forgiveness is cause for unbridled celebration. *His mercy endures forever,*[8] therefore, it is reason enough to dance on forever. I find great joy in the forgiveness of my sins. It is the main reason I love singing the old hymns of redemption.

Wonderful grace of Jesus, greater than all my sin,

How shall my tongue describe it?

Where shall its praise begin?[9]

If we are to forgive we must first revel in the forgiveness granted us. We must first celebrate the great love wherewith we are loved. Paul exhorts, *"rejoice always,"*[10] because we are always forgiven. He says, *"rejoice evermore,"*[11] because we are evermore forgiven. Delighted by God's forgiveness, we can pass it on.

Passing the Torch

During the 2008 Olympics in Beijing, China, the American track team was heavily favored to win the 400-meter relay. They had dominated the race at past Olympics, winning seventeen of the twenty-one times the event occurred. It appeared they would win again until they dropped the baton and fell hopelessly behind the rest of the field. The receiving runner said, "By the time I went to grab it, there was nothing." Like contestants in a relay race, we must firmly grasp the baton before we can run with it. God extends the baton of pardon to us; we grasp it, and run with it to other waiting hands. As Paul says, *"Let us run with patience the race that is set before us."*12 Let us take the time to fully grasp the marvelous forgiveness that Jesus passes to us. Otherwise, like the devastated athlete, we may lament, "By the time I went to forgive, there was nothing."

Setting great store on His forgiveness we store up love for God. We prepare to forgive by basking in the light of His love who forgave us. Before we excuse others, we embrace mercy. We first celebrate God's grace, and then we share it. When we know that we are gloriously forgiven, we are ready to forgive.

Like the weeping harlot who washed Jesus' feet with tears, or the astonished prophet who dared not touch even the Lord's shoelaces, His kindness opens our hearts to the world. Before we attempt to forgive, let us first bask in His mercy and be thankful. The more worshipful we are for the mercy shown us the more forgiving we shall be.

Now, let us look upon the compassion of our King...

1Luke 1:15-16; 2Matthew 11:11; 3John 1:21; 4Mark 1:7; 5Luke 1:78; 6John 3:29; 7Romans 4:7,8; 8Psalm 106:2; 9Wonderful Grace of Jesus by H Lillenas; 10Philippians; 4:4; 111Thessalonians 5:16; 12Hebrews 12:1

Jeff Quill

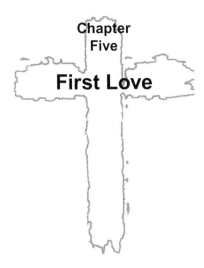

Chapter Five

First Love

We love him, because He first loved us. 1John 4:19

O ne of my favorite old hymns is the cheery Count Your Blessings by Johnson Oatman. I especially like these lines:

Count your blessings; name them one by one.

Count your blessings; see what God hath done.

He goes on to explain that taking time to count your blessings lifts your heart and shakes off your doubt, worry, and sadness. It picks you up and puts you in a positive frame of mind.

It's like counting stars. When we first started counting them eons ago, the most we could see at one time was three thousand. Galileo came along with his telescope and suddenly we had thirty thousand. As our telescopes improve, the count rises until now we've pretty much decided it's a lost cause. So it is with the blessings of God's forgiveness. The more we count, the more we discover. I heard a verse added to Oatman's hymn by an old country preacher. He sang:

Count your blessing name them o'er and o'er

And it will surprise you there are thousands more.

These blessings you count are yours through the forgiveness of God. Seeing how great His love is for you ignites your

17

love for Him. Those blessings are like a deep well of refreshing mercy; what we draw from it we share with others. We forgive others from a boundless reservoir of the Love Who first forgave us. We are not forgiven because we are so utterly merciful; we are merciful because we are so utterly forgiven. For a fuller appreciation of God's love, let's tally up a few blessings of His forgiveness.

I remember well my first conscious contact with that forgiving love. I'll start my count with that story... In my youth well-meaning nuns vividly described for me the torments that awaited bad boys like me. My catechism featured pen and ink drawings of tormented souls. Barely visible through dancing flames and billowing smoke, they screamed, wide-eyed, with arms reaching for mercy that would never come. The poor souls in purgatory did not fare much better: they stood in waist high flames, hands devoutly folded, patiently awaiting deliverance. The thought of a flaming hell (or purgatory if I was lucky) sickened my soul. What chance did a wretch like me stand to escape this horrific fate? In my late teens, whenever friends asked, "Hey, Jeff, where you going?" I always flippantly replied, "To hell if I don't change my ways. Ha. Ha." Any one who cared to listen could have heard the lurking fear in my shallow laughter.

O Happy Day

One memorable night, sitting at a kitchen table, talking with a friend about what "life" is – I became aware of God all around us in the room. He was as real to me as the air I was breathing or the stark naked light from the ceiling bulb. Just the fact that He would visit me in that crummy one room apartment flooded my soul with joy and love. Yet even after He awakened my faith, like many other believers, I still feared all the *hell* talk in the book of Matthew. But

T'was grace that taught my heart to fear

And Grace my fears relieved[1]

A couple of weeks later, January first, with just the clothes on my back, I set out hitch hiking across America. Like so many young "Jesus Freaks" of that day, I was out to find my God, work my way to heaven, and save my sorry soul. I made it all the way to the Sandia Mountains of New Mexico before I got myself in real trouble. With severely frost bitten feet, I ended up in an Albuquerque hospital. I had plenty of time to read my Bible since I could not stand or walk.

One long bed ridden day, I received a visit from a Christian worker named Ralph; an old Mennonite tinsmith from Linden, Alberta, out traveling the world, preaching the gospel to one soul at a time. He began to gently guide my studies, lending me a book called <u>The Gospel of Grace</u>.2 Ah, the weight that lifted the day I read and understood the words, *"Very truly, I say to you, he that believes on Me **has** everlasting life."*3

O, I believed, and I knew then beyond all doubt, that for me there would be no hellfire or gnashing of teeth in outer darkness, isolated from God. It was a light-burst of forgiveness staggering me with inexpressible gladness. Like so many surprised by this love, I was overcome with sheer, mad joy. Many figured me for a fanatic. Maybe I was. It was all I could talk about for months. What other topic can compare to the love of my Jesus? While I manage to chat about the mundane now, I still think everything is dull conversation compared to the loving-kindness of God.

The Rescuer

The better we understand the catastrophe hanging over us, the more we adore the Rescuer and treasure His pardon.

I've heard three different stories of men miraculously rescued from cliffs while hiking alone in the woods. One, spread eagle on a near vertical bolder, called to God and found himself standing again above the drop. Another, hanging from a small root, took the hand of a stranger. When he reached level ground, there was no one in sight who could have extended the hand. Another tripped on a tree root in the dark and fell to the ground. Had he taken two more steps, he would have fallen to his death. He gave his live to the God who saved it.

But God saved them and you and me from much worse. I stumbled toward the edge of the bottomless pit – Jesus pulled me away and into His arms. He washed away my sin. I don't know how this happened, but I felt perfectly clean and clear. Countless new believers say that same thing, "I feel so clean!" It's marvelous to hear, but what is that? It is the sound of the forgiven; the song of a soul set free.4 It is the sigh of first love.

As though raised from the dead, I felt alive, whole, and bright. How else can I describe it but to say, "I was filled with the Spirit." The whole world was infant green. To this day, when I draw close to my heavenly Father, I still sense the newness of all things. A tree I saw a thousand times before, is there for the first time. To share with me the wonder of it all, He opens my eyes to the beauty around me. What a sweet love. What delicious forgiveness.

Counting Sparrows

Our Lord counts His blessings too. You are one of them. Like a man counting his treasure, He counts hairs on your undeserving head. He who fusses over flowers and dotes over fallen sparrows[5] says to you, *"Don't be scared away, you bear more value than great flocks of sparrows."*[6] I fancy Him saying that with a wink, knowing what He was willing to pay. But forget countless sparrows, He thinks you are of greater value than the whole world.

He said, *"What does it profit a man, if gaining the whole world, he loses his own soul? What shall a man trade for his soul?"*[7] He said this fully prepared to barter blood in answer to His own question.

A world war two fighter pilot bailed out over the Pacific as his plane went down. Natives of the nearby island picked him out of the water, and traded him to a U.S. friendly tribe. He later said, "Not many people can tell you what they are worth, but I can. I'm worth just what they got for me – a ten pound sack of rice." Christ respectfully disagrees. He willingly traded His life because He believes that no one and no thing in the whole universe can take your place in His heart.

If someone pays a lot for something, they take especially good care of it. He is deeply invested in you and so His interests in you are only good. His every action toward you is a deliberate calculation of unbounded love. *"I know the plans I devise for you,"* says the LORD, *"plans of prosperous peace, and not misery, to give you things hoped for in the end."*[8]

As our Jewish brothers and sisters sing:
If He had done all this and no more, dayenu!

[1]Amazing Grace– John Newton; [2]B.G,Leonard; [3]John 6:47; [4]Tis the Song Of A Soul Set Free– Oswald J. Smith; [5]Luke 12:27,28, Matthew 10:29; [5]Matthew 10:31; [6]Mark 8:36; [7]Jeremiah 29:11; [8]Dayenu– traditional Jewish folk song. The word means, "That would have been enough."

Chapter Six

His

*Behold, what manner of love the Father hath bestowed upon us, that we should be called the sons of God.*1John 3:1

You are more than someone with a fresh outlook on the world. You are more than just a person with a new lease on life; you are **His** baby – you are **His** newborn. Because you are forgiven, you are now His son; and you now are His daughter. Sure, you are saved from a wrath reserved for His enemies, but more – you are made a child of the Most High God. Isn't He everyone's Father? Well yes. In the sense that He is our maker, just as Thomas Edison is father of the light bulb, or like Jubal in the book of Genesis, *He was the **father** of all who play the harp and flute.*1 You said, "Yes, Lord," to His mercy, as a result, you are His own darling child held close to His heart. It is personal, very personal.

You may have this feeling: "Who am I to come into the house of God and ask for anything?" Who indeed. Who are you to come into His presence? You are His Child. You are His friend. You are the one for whom Christ died, the redeemed one, washed in the blood of the lamb. You are the one Jesus loves, the one in whom He lives. You are the one He forgave, the one He saved. You are **that** one. That is who you are. He wants to be with you – keep company with you – spend time with you. You are God's precious

23

child, and God is your loving Father; His heart warms at your voice calling, *"Abba, (Papa) Father".*2 You are His girl; you are His boy. You are His kid – His forgiven kid: His pride, and joy. You are His everything now and forever. An early church father said, "We are God's joy, His reward, His glory, His crown."

This is the comedy that scandalizes the world. He allows folks like us into His presence; inviting us with a fearsome passion, shedding His very blood to let us in. We come because we believe this blood to be greater than our sin. We come because He calls us, and because He calls us friends. We come because we are children of the Light. We come because this kindness compels us. It is a kindness doting on the littlest of things, and constantly contemplating the weighty issues of our life. It is worth our while to continue listing the mercies of Him who devotedly counts heartbeats, measures every breath, and constantly broods over our life and death.

Heirs

*The Spirit itself bears witness with our spirit, that we are the children of God: And if children, then heirs; heirs of God, and joint-heirs with Christ.*3

This means that the entirety of what God is, and all that He owns is yours. His wealth is your wealth. All He possesses is yours. From the smallest, quickest electron to the largest lumbering galaxy, all is yours. You won't get your mind around this, but the Word declares, *"All things are yours; whether… the world, or life, or death, or things present, or things to come; all are yours and you are Christ's; and Christ is God's."*4 It is all yours because you are lovingly forgiven.

Once upon a time, a King went riding alone through his kingdom. Deep in a forest he came to a rickety bridge over a raging mountain stream. Gently he urged his horse forward out over the water, when suddenly another rider broke from the trees near the other end of the bridge. Waving a sword over his head, he charged toward the King. It was a woodland robber intent on killing the royal. The attacker's horse hit the slick wobbly planks and its hooves shot out from underneath, throwing the killer headfirst onto the deck, over the side and unconscious into the violent river. The King leaped from his horse into the water and caught up to the drowning man, grabbed him by the collar and dragged him ashore. He took the man home and tended to him for days.

When the thief awoke, he was in a large bed in an enormous room of a splendid castle with hundreds of servants. A kindly gentleman assisted him in dressing, and escorted him to the dining hall. There stood the King. The criminal began to shake knowing he was doomed. Before he could fall to his knees and beg for mercy, the Monarch embraced him.

"Good morning friend," he said. "Come have breakfast with me, and after that, if you so choose, you may live here as my son for the rest of your life and own all that you see."

Your salvation through forgiveness is like that. You are not just pulled from the water; you are given a life and a hope in mansions of love and holiness. His mercy buys your heart back from death and bitterness, and makes it a conduit of His love. You are a rebel ransomed from the hell of hatred and appointed an *ambassador*5 of the King of Love.

Thine and Mine

From the love song of Solomon: *"My Beloved is mine, and I am His."*6 I own God's heart and He owns mine. The Most Merciful God gives Himself to me in the form of His Son, Jesus Christ. From the hymn writer Fanny Crosby:

Blessed assurance, Jesus is mine.

O What a foretaste of glory divine.

With forgiveness God gives Himself to me. He is mine. He is yours.

The gardener at Sacred Heart Convent told me he overheard the nuns as they worked among the roses. One looked about at the beautiful spring day and said, "Oh my Jesus."

At which another stood up and gently chided, "Oh no, Sister, **My** Jesus."

One after another they chimed in, "**My** Jesus."

"No, **My** Jesus."

I've met many believers who feel the same way. One dear old friend of mine said, "You know what I find so amazing? With all the love He gives me, He still has enough for anyone else. But He does. Just as much, too. He loves me infinitely and He loves you infinitely at the same time. Can you imagine that?"

His love is so intense and immense it seems you are His one and only. You are forever His. You are forgiven, and you belong to Him. This wondrous love compels surrender. No longer an enemy, you are the precious child of your Abba, the King. For His excessive love, too much is not nearly enough. He continues to lavish blessing on you...

Blameless

The apostle says, *"God...has blessed us with all spiritual blessings in heavenly places in Christ: even as He has chosen us in Him before the foundation of the world, that we should be holy and without blame in the sight of His love."*[7] It was His plan from the start of time to make us His own, and bless us with all He had, to cherish us, and hold us blameless before His eyes. He will tolerate no accusation against us. He will silence the voice of our accuser, Satan, forever. He holds us beyond suspicion for all eternity. He will see to it that His vision of us proves true in the end. From the first day of creation, nothing was going to get in His way. *He that spared not his own Son, but delivered him up for us all, how shall he not with him also freely give us all things?*[8] Nothing will stop Him now. The word "give" in this verse (Charizomai) can also be translated "forgive." God is intimating that His giving all things comes with His forgiving all things. What love!

Ages Upon Ages

"God, who is rich in mercy, because of His great love with which He loved us, even when we were dead in sins, made us alive together with Christ. It is by grace we are saved."[9] And here is why He did it: *So that in the ages to come He will show the infinite wealth of His grace in His kindness toward us through Christ Jesus.*[9] God, by His great love for us, made us alive, so He could show us His kindness for ages to come. Think of that feeling you get watching joy cover the face of a child as she opens a gift from you. Wrapping-paper and ribbons fly, the lid opens, and then the face beams with a light that comes from knowing she is loved. The hug around the neck is pretty good too. That is God's big thrill, forever watching us open His gift and lift our arms to Him in perpetual delight.

Eternities of kindness have come upon you. Through age upon age of wonder, love, and joy, you will see and experience fresh marvels. It is a far flight beyond your comprehension – yet fully apprehended for you. That is much too much to count, but He just cannot stop. He cannot help Himself. His love for you spurs Him on to limitless showers of blessing...

1Genesis 4:21; 2Galatians 4:6; 3Romans 8:16-17; 41Corinthians 3:21-23; 52Corinthians 5:20; 6Song of Solomon 2:16; 7Ephesians 1: 3-4; 8Romans 8:32; 9Ephesians 2: 4-7

Jeff Quill

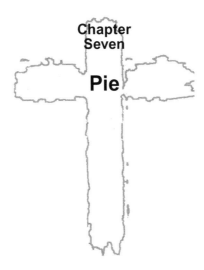

Chapter Seven

Pie

In the ages to come He will show the immeasurable wealth of His grace. Ephesians 2:7

It will take forever to unpack the treasure that now lives in your heart. The wealth that is yours through God's forgiveness will unfold for all eternity. As wonderful as that may be, He is not just serving up some "pie in the sky when you die."[1] He wants to fill your plate now. Scripture says that the Holy Spirit of promise, who has come to live in your heart, is *The guarantee deposit of our inheritance.*[2] That means money down or earnest money on His eternal wealth. In a real estate sale, earnest money is just a fraction of the value of the property the buyer pays the seller. In the kingdom of heaven things are all turned around: up and down are backwards and left and right are inside out. Christ is the seller, Christ is the buyer, but Christ gives the deposit to you.

Doing The Math

Consider the value of a fraction of what the indwelling Spirit means for you. According to Gracie over at Gossard's Roadhouse, the average size of a piece of pie is twelve point five percent, or one eighth of the whole. What is one eighth of infinity? By my calculations, it is still infinity. My silliness here is just to point out how big this is. The Spirit of God is your piece of the pie now.

Like dogs, we settle for crumbs under the table when God wants to lavish the unimaginable upon us. Looking at the state of our world you have to wonder: what are we missing?

I knew a young man who had dreamed a dream in which he arrived in heaven and was escorted to his eternal home. Opening the door of the mansion, he saw stacks of colorfully wrapped boxes of every size. They filled the rooms so that there was barely space enough to move about.

"What's all this?" he asked?

The angel replied, "These are gifts the Lord sent you when you lived on earth. They all came back unopened so we stored them here."

What great things does He want to give us now? How much more does He have for us today? Paul says it is *super abundantly beyond all we can ask or think.*[3] Which of course, includes the virtue of forgiveness. Even if forgiving is super abundantly more than we think possible, it is ours for the opening. He goes on to call our portion, *"the unsearchable riches of Christ – that eye has not seen nor ear heard neither has entered into the heart of man: things that God has prepared for them that love Him."*[4]

Them that love Him are we who stand here soaked in the downpour of His grace. The things awaiting us will keep us blinking in the light of wonder forever. He does all this for us who were once His enemies. This love bewilders any rational expectation. It is extreme, extravagant forgiveness.

Doggéd Blessings

His desire and intent is to pile blessings on blessings. He tells Abraham, *"That in blessing I will bless you."*[5] In other words, "I will bless your blessings. I will stack blessing on top of blessing on top of blessing." This is His will. This is what He wants to do. His Torah pronounces this upon you: *"Blessed shall you be in the city, and blessed in the field. Blessed your basket and bowl. Blessed shall you be when you come in, and blessed when you go out."*[6]

You are to be blessed wherever you are; no matter what church you attend, or don't attend. God watches over you in the city and He works along side you in the field. His love waits for you at home to bring peace under your roof, and follows you to work to prosper the work of your hands. As the shepherd-poet said, *"Surely goodness and mercy shall follow me all the days of my life."*7 The Lord commands His happiness and favor to stay close to you like a couple of loyal sheep dogs. At this very moment, His blessing is seeking a way into your day. Yet you see only a faint, distant outline of the mountainous bounty He has for you. You accepted His forgiveness, and ever so much more comes with that. Count this:

The Heritage of Forgiveness

You are His child; what is His is yours. But for now, just look at this one particular blessing: the ability to forgive. The element of forgiveness is His; therefore, it also is yours. It is your birthright to forgive because you inherit His great forgiving heart.

Some traits run in families. This trait of forgiveness runs in your family. You look at a baby and say, "Oh, he has his father's chin. Poor fellow." Your God wants to hear people say, "Oh, she has her Father's heart. He has his Fathers mercy." Forgiveness is your heritage. Whether or not you can see it in yourself, your Abba sees it in you. He is delighted with you.

Let's tally up more of this enormous love:

Home

Though you have an eternal place in His heart, He has also prepared a heavenly place. *In my Father's house are many homes… I go to prepare a place for you. And if I go and prepare a place for you, I will come again, and receive you unto myself, that where I am, there you may be also.*8 He built a home just so He could be with you. Will you agree with me that however glorious that mansion may be, it can in no way compare to the beauty of your God? It is nothing when set beside the possibility of taking a quiet walk alone with your Jesus, down some serene foot path in heaven. Even now, even here, there are precious moments He longs to share with you. You, in particular, are dear to His heart.

Your Heavenly Father's love for you is unspeakable, incomprehensible, and forever just beginning. He has His prophet tell you, *"The Lord your God is with you, and He is a mighty savior.*

31

He will rejoice in you with gladness; He will rest you in His love,
He will tremble in joy over you with singing."[9]

Someday you will hear God singing a love song He wrote about you, inspired by the joy of watching you forgive. It may go something like this:

You are altogether beautiful, My love.
There is no flaw in you."[10]

That's how He sees it. And the more He forms His forgiveness in you, the more you too will see things that way.

But I must ask you, "What did all this cost your God?"...

[1]The Preacher and the Slave– Joe Hill; [2]Ephesians 1:14; [3]Ephesians 3:20; [4]1Corinthians 2:9; [5]Genesis 22:17; [6]Deuteronomy 28:3,6; [7]Psalms 23:6; [8]John 14:2-3; [9]Zephaniah3:17; [10]Song of Solomon 4:7

Jeff Quill

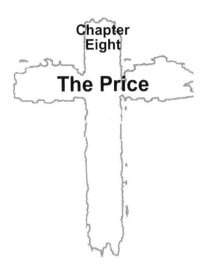

Chapter Eight

The Price

A dealer in high priced antiques was invited to dinner at the humble home of a family friend. During the course of the evening he saw on the bookshelf an extremely rare first edition by a famous author. He asked the host if he would be willing to sell it.

"No sir. That's been in this family for hundreds of years. I am a descendant of that author. It was his personal copy, and his signature is on the title page along with notes about his writing."

The dealer continued to badger his poor friend throughout the evening. Finally the host named a price for the book that was at least a thousand times its worth – a sum that could easily bankrupt the antique dealer.

"That's just crazy," said the would-be book buyer.

"Well, I'm just crazy about that book," answered the host.

Appraisals

The price we put on something shows how much it means to us. The things Jesus willingly suffered for us reveal how God cherishes us; how highly He values us. By any reasonable human standard one would have to say, "God is just crazy about you." In the New Testament, one preacher says that when sophisticated

35

people heard the outrageous price Jesus paid for them, they considered it *the foolishness of God.*₁

Eternal mercy is not cheap. It comes at a steep price that could easily bankrupt the world: the suffering and death of God's only begotten Son. Forgiveness is love; it is a costly love. You can glimpse the immense forgiveness bestowed upon you by viewing your huge debt and its great cost to God.

If our hold on His love is feeble, it is because we are unaware of the danger we faced before we trusted Him. We do not understand the fury checked, and the agony spared us, and most importantly, the toll our sin took on Jesus Christ.

How big was our spiritual and moral debt? As we saw in the wicked servant story, a very small debt could mean prison if a creditor pressed his rights. The Bible says that we are *debtors to the whole Law*₂ and *Whoever keeps the whole law and yet stumbles at just one point is guilty of breaking all of it.*₃ This means that every debt is an enormous debt. Every little bit owed is a deficit exposing us to unthinkable consequences. The horrendous cost of our pardon shows what a threat the least of our sins is to us. Without His forgiveness, we are looking at this grand total on our final invoice: a lost eternity.

Offended Justice Called for Blood.

"The soul who sins shall die," and *"without the shedding of blood there is no remission,"*₄ declare the apostles and prophets. In the Old Testament we read that the blood of innocent animals was offered to temporarily offset guilt. These ritual killings plainly lay out for us the un-payable cost of sin. Slaughtered animals in the ancient temple at Jerusalem were foreshadowing symbols of the sinless Christ – that Moses called, *"a lamb without blemish."*₅ Only His innocent blood restores innocence to our guilty souls and only His life without defect can redeem our defective lives. Our death will not correct the underlying moral imbalance because, as Scripture tells us, we are already *dead in trespasses and sins.*₆ The offer of guilty blood only makes things worse. Void of life, it is unacceptable atonement. We possess no remedy for injured justice. God ordered His prophet to say, *"I have no pleasure in the death of the wicked but that the wicked turn from his way and live."*₇

Seeing that we could not possibly pay, God sacrificed a Lamb for our sins: He offered Himself for us. *With His own blood He entered the Most Holy Place once for all, having found and seized our eternal redemption. If the blood of goats and bulls and the ashes of a calf can restore purity, how much more, then, will the blood of Christ, who through the eternal Spirit offered Himself unblemished to God?*[8]

This sacrifice is necessary because of the infinite disparity between our fallen nature and God's holiness. It is like the difference between a living fire, immeasurably bigger and hotter than the sun, and a tiny, dead, rotted twig. How can you get these two things together and still have both? Something has to burn. Christ became (again in the words of Moses) *the burnt offering.*[9]

All In

Our God spared no expense to spare us the expense of our sin. He avoided no pain to lift us from utter doom up to uttermost favor, from the everlasting death to eternal life. When we picture the scene of His crucifixion, we picture what divine justice held for us if not for the interference of Jesus' inexplicable love. He worked out the solution to the fire of holiness and the wrath of justice by taking it into His own hands through excruciating nails.

When you look at Christ crucified – Jesus on the cross – you are looking at the wrath of God poured out upon you. You are witnessing your second death. *It is appointed to everybody once to die, but after that there is judgment.*[10]

John the Revelator paints a gruesome image. (Without Christ, this could be any or all of us.) *"But the fearful, and unbelieving, and the abominable, and murderers, and whoremongers, and sorcerers, and idolaters, and all liars shall have their part in the lake, which burns with fire and brimstone: which is the second death."*[11] This is why God became a man: so He could taste the second death for you. When your judgment fell upon Christ it was like He swallowed a lake of fire.

In The Book of Revelation (The Apocalypse) we find a hint of what that tastes like. It is the recipe for what John calls, a *cup of-fierce-wrath-and-indignation-wine*: sudden worldwide plagues of pain, disease, and infestation, pollution, catastrophic weather, drought, earthquake, and unprecedented war. Filled with terror, *every island flees away, and the mountains are not found.*12 Is it any wonder Jesus' sweat was like *great drops of blood* as He prayed, *"O My Abba, if it be possible let this cup pass from Me."*13

And yet He took that cup. Though He begged to be spared, He went on to swallow death for me and for you. Why did He do that?...

1Corinthians 1:25; 2Galatians 5:3; 3James 2:10; 4Ezekiel 18:20, Hebrews 9:22; 5Exodus 12:5; 6Ephesians 2:1; 7Ezekiel 33:11; 8Hebrews9:13,14;9Leviticus1:4;10Hebrews9: 27;11Revelation21:812Revelation 16:19-20; 13Luke 22:44, Matthew 26:3

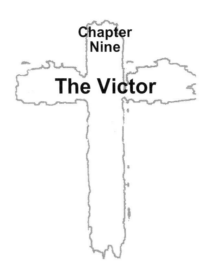

Chapter Nine

The Victor

I worked in a factory alongside a fellow who hated God. He used to say, "I'm going to hell because that's where all the fun is." Seems like a joke, but unfortunately he was serious. He refused to believe that Hell was something other than a rowdy vacation spot.

I tried to explain, "No, heaven is the fun place, Hell is the place of boredom and eternal dissatisfaction. The party is in heaven. No one enjoys anything in hell." But he would not hear of it, and wanted none of my Savior. Maybe he had resigned himself to it because he knew he did not deserve to be in heaven. Other than Jesus, no one is in heaven who deserves to be there; there is no one in hell that doesn't deserve to be there. Though I am worthy of hell, God's forgiveness will land me in heaven. That's a blessing stacked high with blessings too numerous to count.

Look at this punishment we were spared. There is much debate about what Hell is. Some people doubt it exists, (That sounds great, but I wouldn't bet my soul on it), while others believe it to be a place of fiery torment. Still others suggest it is a spiritual state of isolation and separation from God. Whatever the case, we can agree it is a horrific prospect. But it is not for you, child of God – you are forgiven. The forgiveness of God in Christ raises you above condemnation and beyond the reach of hell;

41

*out of darkness into his marvelous light.*1 You shall pass through gates brighter than hope, into the warm embrace of your waiting Father. He forever eliminates any threat of eternal damnation for all who trust the Son of the Living God. You are forgiven. You are loved. You are safeguarded in the heart of The Almighty.

Trading Places.

He took the consequence of your actions in trade for the consequence of His actions. At the judgment seat of Christ you will see this. He will show what He has done in you and what you have done in Him. You will be surprised at how eager He is to celebrate you. No one is going to humiliate you. All is forgiven. Every sin, every great and heinous crime, every vague notion of will, every deliberate, out and out offence, and flat felony is dismissed. Nothing will be held against you in the court of Heaven. When you stand before the Judge of all the earth and the record books of your offences are opened, the pages will be indecipherable. At the reading of the charges silence shall fill the great hall.

The prosecution will announce, *"This is Jesus, King of the Jews."*2 The pages will be unreadable because His blood blotted them out.

In the Apostles creed we say, "He descended into hell." The Hebrew word for Hell is "Sheol." It is the hole of eternal death. Jesus descended lower than that. Under Him was only Himself. Dying deeper than all death, He obliterates mortality.

Dying our death, He *emptied Himself*3 of divine likeness and human dignity. He poured out his soul unto death,4 creating a spiritual vacuum of such force that it took away the sin of the whole world. He discarded His life, drained His blood, and absorbed all into Himself, turning the universe inside out through the unbounded sacrifice of His holy life. The moral imbalance, tilting everything, slides the whole of creation into His arms. It is the irresistible vortex of divine love. Thus your Savior gives up everything for you: *Behold the Lamb of God who takes away the sin of the whole world.*5

His obedience unto the death draws like a limitless spiritual tornado. *The LORD has His way in the whirlwind and in the storm, and the clouds are the dust of His feet...the earth is carried away at His presence, yes, the world, and all that dwell therein.*6 Jesus alludes to this storm of divine Love's ferocity saying, *"the king-dom of heaven suffers violence, and the violent take it by force."*[7] The cross of Christ, like a hurricane of love, takes the kingdom for us. By faith in his blood, we ride, as the old hymnodist says, "the wings of the storm,"[8] into Heaven. The pinnacle, the depths, and the whole of existence, wisp into the fatally wounded savior. Bleeding out, the Christ exhales with a final shout of triumph, *"It is finished."*[9]

His death inhales the universe and God Himself.[10] We are all swept into Christ, and meet our searching Father there. With all our counting, let's count this: *God has not appointed us to wrath, but to obtain salvation by our Lord Jesus Christ.*[11] Our God appointed us to life and the splendor of His forgiveness.

Now let's talk about who it is that we, the joyously forgiven, are to forgive...

[1]Peter 2:9; [2]Matthew 27:37; [3]Philippians 2:7,8; [4]Isaiah 53:12; [5]John 1:29; [6]Amos 1:14; [7]Matthew 11:12; [8]O Worship the King by Robert Grant; [9]John19:30; [10]2Corinthians5:19, Colossians 2:9; [11]1Thessalonians 5:9

Chapter
Ten
Forgive Us Our Virtues

Before we move further, let us look at who and what needs forgiveness. It is not always so clear. For instance, if I am offended by the action of someone in the right, how can I presume to forgive him or her for doing the right thing? The fact that they were in the right gets in the way. Let's remove this obstacle.

Every day my drive to work took me down a winding hill. I was careful because right at the bottom of the hill was a bus stop where the children often seemed to be running about, not paying attention. I always rode the brakes to keep from exceeding the low speed limit on my descent. One particular morning, knowing the bus stop would be abandoned for summer break, I let the car coast and pick up speed, sparing my brakes. The children were replaced that morning with a patrolman looking for drivers sparing their brakes. After years of caution on that street, pulled over at the bus stop in front of red and blue flashing lights, I confess, I tried to make the officer miserable in His task. He was courteous and fair and certainly deserved an apology. Having done nothing wrong, did he need to be forgiven for his actions? The surprising answer is, "Yes." That may sound sociopathic, so allow me to explain.

45

Doing Right

Parents enacting necessary discipline can suffer rejection for years or even for life. I may seethe over a reprimand I deserved from my employer, or resent a tax collector for doing his job, or a teacher for failing me. The fact that my adversary is in the right does little to soothe my wounded pride. No, forgiveness is not meant to pacify my ruffled ego, but it may help me to let go of sour feelings. But why should someone be forgiven for what they do right? Some hurts come to us deservedly, making it hard to forgive.

Folks just going about everyday living can unintentionally bruise our pride. What of a competitor? Feelings about business run deep, and deeper still on something as inconsequential as amateur sport. At a rival university campus, a fanatical fan poisoned a beloved one hundred thirty-year-old oak tree around which students traditionally gathered to celebrate victories.1 Though the winning school was innocent of any wrongdoing, they may have preferred unwarranted forgiveness to undeserved revenge. That criminal probably sat in his prison cell wishing he knew how to forgive his guiltless opponent.

The best of what we do and the best of who we are needs to be forgiven. A friend of mine surrendered her life to Christ when she realized, "I could do no right. No matter what good I did it turned our to be hurtful to someone." Even our kindness is not always helpful, and sometimes harmful. Every touch that is from less than the hands of Christ is imperfect.

And a certain woman, (whom Jesus healed) *had an issue of blood twelve years, And had suffered many things of many physicians, and had spent all that she had, and was nothing bettered, but rather grew worse.*2

Our strongest examples of wisdom and compassion, like doctors, teachers, and ministers, buckle under the weight of inherent weakness. The most honorable things done and said by the most honored souls fall sadly short of God's ideal. Isaiah claims, *"We are all as an unclean thing, and all our righteousnesses are as filthy rags."*3 That means even our good stuff is bad. **Righteousness-es** are good characteristics, qualities, and acts. Christ died not only for the things we do wrong, but also for the things we think we do right. He gave His life to atone for the best we do and finest we are.

Good People

My Aunt Kay saw my picture in a newspaper article meant to raise funds for St. Joseph's Orphanage. Shocked to find that I lived there, she came to visit me. Eventually, she took me into her home. At fifty-two, she had little experience with children. Now, along with menopause, came a culture shocked fifteen-year-old, neurotic waif. My move from the calm order of the orphanage into the wild chaos of the nineteen sixties was hard on me, and ever so much harder on her. She did all she could to help. I resented her efforts, and we clashed often as she tried to protect me from myself.

I know the fiery, Irish redhead would laugh if she knew I was telling you that she was a saint. Still, this kindness that makes me love the memory of my sainted Aunt Kay, needs to be redeemed. Of course this is hard to hear, and even harder to accept, but it must be said. It's OK to pardon the loving kindness of our imperfect heroes. We need to know that it is all right to forgive **good** people for doing what seem to be good things.

The Philosopher of Ecclesiastes muses, *"Better is a poor and a wise child than an old and stupid king, who will no more be admonished."*4 My anger over correction is the stupid reaction of fearful pride. I want control. I want to be the King of Me. When I forgive the disciplinarian, I can then become as a wise child. I gain the benefit of instruction by humbling myself.

Altars

In Old Testament days, even something so right as thanksgiving, or any approach to God, required a blood sacrifice. This suggests that our most sublime action – worship – must be redeemed. The temple altar itself had to be sanctified, with the blood of sacrifice. In other words it had to be set apart and cleansed from its contact with sinful man.

*Seven days you shall make atonement for the altar, and sanctify it.*5

The altar represents our religions, philosophies, platforms of faith, and mechanisms of good work. Christ must atone for them all; *"For my thoughts are not your thoughts, neither are your ways* my ways," says the Lord. "For as the heavens are higher than the earth, so are my ways higher than your ways, and my thoughts than your thoughts."6 God's goodness is brighter than ours as a star is brighter than a black hole. Our shiniest virtue can no more stand beside His holiness than a bee's-wax candle on the sun.

Good Behavior

We like to justify our lives by our good conduct, our worth-while endeavors, and our right living. The cross of Christ offends us because it says our virtuous behavior is not enough to make up for our wrongs; it says that our little sin (little to us) is big enough to call for such a drastic punishment. According to Saints James and John, "Sin is the transgression of the law." and the least offence – the slightest misstep – makes us "guilty of all."7 Stepping ten inches off the edge of a cliff is as good as leaping ten feet off that cliff, once you hit the rocks below. The Lord's death demonstrates the severity of our debt. An invoice written across His brow with thorns asserts that we have an incalculable moral debt to pay. We may bristle when told that our sin is so bad it requires the blood of the Son of God. This is the offense of the cross.8 It is why Jesus declares, "Blessed is he, whosoever shall not be offended in Me."9

Christ's death for sin affronts good people, and rattles the delicate sensibilities of our finest citizens. Such retribution is for the filth, the PolPots, Amins, and Stalins that perpetrated the genocides of the twentieth century. How can we be compared to them?

Charm Is Deceptive. Proverbs 31:30

I saw some beautiful watercolor landscapes painted by an obscure Austrian artist. Surely anyone capable of such beauty must be a wonderful person. Then it was revealed that the artist was a young man named Adolf Hitler. Though we present with grace and beauty we are all vulnerable to the evil deep within. The Bible warns us, "Satan himself is transformed into an angel of light. Therefore it is no great thing if his ministers also be trans-formed as the ministers of righteousness."10 Most of us struggle with the notion that at our best we may be agents of darkness. This frightening idea should be enough to send us running to the arms of our Savior.

48

Good Intentions

In 1961 a prominent university conducted an experiment in which volunteers, using a microphone, quizzed a person listening from another room. The test taker responded to the yes or no questions by turning on a red or green light. If the listener answered incorrectly, a lab-coated, clipboard-toting attendant ordered the questioner to press a button that gave an electric shock to the person in the other room. With each wrong answer the voltage increased. Unknown to the questioners, no current was actually sent; no one was actually shocked. After several wrong answers, the test taker began to groan, pretending to beg for mercy from the other room. None of the participants believed they would ever obey orders from an authority figure like Hitler, but "for the greater good, and the advancement of knowledge," most of them administered what would have been seriously harmful and sometimes lethal jolts.[11] This cruel and sadistic experiment was unnecessary because the Bible informs everyone, *"The heart is deceitful above all things, and desperately wicked: who can know it?*[12] *Their feet are swift to shed blood. Destruction and misery are in their ways."*[13] We all stand in need of mercy. We are all equally guilty in the shadow of the cross.

It's not my brother or my sister but it's me,

O Lord, a-standin' in the need of prayer.[14]

Though none of this yet explains how to forgive, it shows that anything is worth forgiving. If you have suffered little or much from the good others did to you, feel free to forgive them.

But first let's see what that forgiveness looks like...

1Toomer's Corner at Auburn University, 2011; 2Mark5:26; 3Isaiah64:6; 4Ecclesiastes 4:13; 5Exodus 29:37; 6Isaiah 55:8; 71John 3:4, James 2:10; 8Galatians 5:11; 9Luke 7:23; 102Corinthians11:14; 11Milgram-Yale; 12Jeremiah 17:9; 13Romans 3:16; 14African-American Spiritual Matthew 18:4

Jeff Quill

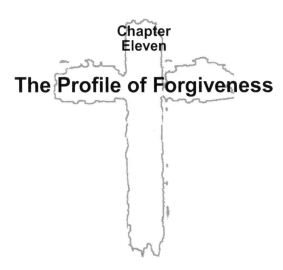

Chapter Eleven
The Profile of Forgiveness

We caught a tiny glimpse of the cost of God's forgiveness, and counted a few blessings that come to us because of it. Now, since this is the forgiveness we hope to find in our hearts, let's see what it looks like.

Holy Amnesia

There is a story of a man who heard the voice of God. When he told his priest about this, the clergyman was skeptical. As a test, he instructed the man, "Ask God what sin I confessed in my last confession."

When next they met the priest asked, "What did God say about my confession?"

The man answered, "He said He doesn't remember." To God it is as if it had never happened.

"They shall all know Me, from the least of them unto the greatest," says the Lord: *"for I will forgive their wickedness and I will remember their sin no more."*[1] One may question, "How can an all-knowing God forget?" The point here is that the misdeeds are not remembered **against** us. The Old Testament describes Abraham's marital betrayal and cowardly lies, but not to revile the man it names, *"The Friend of God."*[2] Scripture relates the story of David's adultery and murder, but not to denounce the one God

51

calls, *"A man after my own heart."*3 If God mentions a forgiven sin, it admonishes the listener, but never condemns or humiliates the pardoned sinner.

The founder of the Red Cross, Clara Barton, forgave a colleague who wronged her. Years later, when a friend reminded her of the incident, she seemed to draw a blank.

"Don't you remember?" asked her friend.

"No," replied Miss Barton, "I distinctly recall forgetting that." She demonstrated her grasp of God's forgiveness and the grasp of God's forgiveness on her.

Lessons

*Whoever was written about in ages past, was written of for our instruction.*4 For instance, the Word records this incident:

On the night of His arrest, Jesus tells Peter, *"Before the rooster crows twice, you will deny me thrice."*5 Later that night, standing by a courtyard fire, Peter swears he never knew Jesus. A rooster crows, and Peter, burning with shame, flees the cold accusing firelight, and weeps bitterly.

After Jesus rises from the dead, He builds a fire on the beach and cooks breakfast for Peter. Standing on the shore with His disciple, perhaps before the rooster could crow, He asks him three times, *"Simon, son of Jonah, do you love me?" Peter was thrown into sorrow because He asked him the third time. And he said unto him, "Lord, You know all things; You know that I love You."* By the warmth of the Lord's fire the old fisherman reaffirms his love once for each denial.6

Peter's old fishing partner, St. John the Evangelist, shares the story to demonstrate the unshakable forgiveness of the resurrected Christ, not to embarrass his good friend. Thus a dark moment in the apostle's life shines for God, enlightening and encouraging us, without disparaging Peter.

Dad

At the opening of this book, prompted of friends, I wrote of my father's drunkenness and abuse. That was hard for me to do because I long ago forgave him, and also I believe it is good to *Honor your father and your mother.*7

But now his struggle is enlisted for the service of Christ. Dad would be happy about that. Even at his life's lowest point he had faith in God. When he heard from family members that I was entertaining atheism, he asked to see me. We talked and drank deep into the night, and at last he said, "Jeffy, I don't often point up, boy," he pointed a finger to the sky, "but I'm pointing up now, I'm pointing up now, I believe, Jeffy. I believe." He was just an ordinary man trapped in a horrible disease. I love him.

Inner Healing

One morning, about fifteen years later, I was meditating on the word "Father" in the Lord's Prayer. I began to think of the day the Catholic Charities came to remove us from my father's house, and take us to the orphanage. It was a painful memory, and my church was teaching that I should try to envision Jesus in painful scenes of my past, so I decided to try it.

Asking the Holy Spirit to help me picture that sad day, I closed my eyes, assuming that I'd see the Savior holding me in His arms. What came to mind surprised me. I saw my dad sitting, legs crossed ankle over knee, his elbow resting on the kitchen table, a cup of instant coffee in his hand. He was trying to smile. Jesus was not standing by me; He was standing behind my father with his hand on the man's shoulder, comforting him at the loss of his children. I knew that Dad was praying, asking Jesus to take care of my siblings and me, to be for us the Father he could not be. He was giving us into the hands of his God. His heart was breaking.

Imagination? Maybe. But I prefer to believe that The Holy Spirit answered my prayer. Though there is no direct scriptural model for this exercise, the Bible does not speak against it, and many have found it helpful. The point is: I want my earthly father remembered as the one who entrusted my heavenly Father with his Jeffy. This episode brought about this song lyric:

My daddy was the son of a broken man,
And I was too young to understand,
When he left me with some folks I didn't know.
But he knew enough by what he heard,
These were people of your word.
He was prayin' I would come to call you,
Abba... Abba, Dadda.
Father above, Father of love.

I have come to love you.
I've come to lean on you.
I've come to look up to you.
Father of the fatherless,
O Papa of tenderness,
Do you know this boy of yours is proud of you?
Abba... Abba, Dadda.
I am so proud of you.[8]

Dad's prayer was answered. More often than not, I call my God, "Papa." By Papa's forgiveness I remember the honor and forget the disgrace.

God's Forgiveness is Opportunistic

Isaiah prophesies this riddle: *"Come now, and let us reason together," says the LORD: "though your sins be as scarlet, they shall be as white as snow; though they be red like crimson, they shall be as wool."*[9]

For one solution to the riddle, note that God does not say, **"You** will be white as snow." He does say, *"**your sins** shall be white."* Christ on the cross took your sin as His own. He paid for it, He owns it, and He forgives it. Your scarlet sin is His to use for His *white as snow* purpose.

This does not mean that your sin is suddenly OK. Never. It simply means that He draws on these crimson failures to cover your life in His wooly-white goodness. His love will use anything and everything in your life and circumstances to bless you. Nothing will go to waste. God now *works all things together for good,*[10] even things that shame you. He uses everything in your world to mold you into the likeness of His forgiving Son. He so thoroughly forgives your sin that He can use it to your advantage. Rather than hold your sins against you, He uses sin against itself to form His tenderheartedness in you.

So, *should we do evil that good may come?*[11] Of course not. Considering the price Jesus had to pay, it hurts to mention such a thing. He is, however, crafting in us a forgiveness so complete, that we will be able to see the good He creates from things we suffer at other's hands. For instance, my father's forgiven failure exposed me to the influence of deep devotion and reverence in the Sisters of Charity. Above all, Mr. & Mrs. Quill's pardoned sins left me with a new Papa – *When my father and my mother forsake me, then the Lord will gather me up.*12

Joseph, sold into slavery by his brothers, becomes Prime Minister of Egypt. When reunited with his brothers he says to them, *"You meant evil against me but God meant it for good."*13 God used the evil deeds of those men to save thousands from starvation. Through the forgiveness God worked in him, Joseph saw the hand of God turning trials into blessings.

Peter tells a crowd in Jerusalem, *"You denied the Holy One… and killed the Prince of Life, whom God hath raised from the dead...and sent Him to bless you in turning each of you away from his iniquities."*14 About five thousand people gave their hearts to Christ the day they heard this.15 Some were the very priests and soldiers involved in the execution of Christ.16 What they meant for evil, God turned to their good. Seizing upon the misdeeds of a few, He saved countless multitudes. In His hands the actions intended for evil brought hope to all. Though their sins were as scarlet, they became white as snow through this magnificent forgiveness.

*How unfathomable are his judgments, and his ways past finding out!*17

But let's keep searching anyway...

1Jeremiah 31:34; 2Genesis, James 2:2312, 2Samuel 11, 3Acts 13:22; 4Romans 15:4; 5Mark 14:30; 6John 21:15-17; 7Exodus 20:12; 8Abba, Dadda: J.Quill; 9Isaiah 1:18; 10Romans 8:28,29; 11Romans 3:8; 12Psalm27:10; 13Genesis50:20; 14Acts 3:26; 15Acts 4:4; 16Acts 6:7; 17Romans 11:33

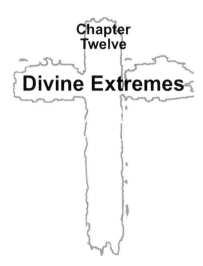

Chapter
Twelve

Divine Extremes

You will cast all our sins into the depths of the sea. Micah 7:19

Mindful that we are looking at the forgiveness God has planted as a seed in our hearts, we continue our tour through God's mercy.

Hopelessly Lost Ships

This metaphor from the prophet Micah, *"depths of the sea"*, is often referred to as the "Sea of God's Forgetfulness." Beyond pearl diving, the people of Micah's day had no underwater experience. Pearl divers descended to a depth of eighty to one hundred twenty-five feet, often at the cost of their lives. Most seafaring men believed the ocean was bottomless. To them it was an infinite, unfathomable abyss, and might as well be so for us. The deepest point in any ocean is about six and a half miles down. The remote camera submarine that found the Titanic some seventy-four years after it sank, goes down less than half that. God is telling us that He submerges our sins into vast, unreachable, ink-black canyons of unconsciousness. Then, for good measure, He buries them.

David, who leaned heavily on God's mercy, declared, *"Happy is he whose transgression is forgiven, whose sin is covered."*[1]

God sinks our sins to inaccessible depths, covering them with the silt of everlasting oblivion – out of reach and out of sight. The only one who could drag them up refuses to look for them because, as the prophet said to Him, *"You are of purer eyes than to view iniquity and unable to gaze upon evil."*[2]

To His thinking, our sins are gone forever. This Sea of His Forgetfulness is the blood pooled at the foot of the cross – the vast, deep purity that drowns the sin of the whole world.[3] There, our sins disappear forever; lost in the blood of the Lamb.

I, even I, am He who blots out your transgressions for My own sake; and I remember not your sins.[4]

Later, we will discuss how this blood is paramount in our ability to forgive. With God's help, we too shall lose track of sins committed against us.

Farther Than Far

As far as the east is from the west, so far has He removed our transgressions from us.[5]

At this writing the nearest sighted galaxy is thirteen billion light years away.[6] Put this same distance in the other direction for a start on catching up with our sin. Add to that, the Psalmist traveled on horseback. The world cannot make enough kite-string to get out there. And He will likewise give us the skill to separate our brothers and sisters from their wrongdoing.

He Forgives Unconditionally

His forgiveness comes with this one stipulation: ask for it. The Psalmist says, *"For You, Lord, are good, and ready to forgive; and plenteous in mercy unto all them that call upon you."*[7] He is ready to forgive anyone who is ready to be forgiven. It is accessible to all who will accept it. It is there for the taking for any who will take it.

Gems of Joy lie about in His presence,
There for the taking by beggars and peasants,
And the residents of the hard road.[8]

His pardon hinges on our plea, not on the condition that we no longer sin. Jesus defended an adulteress facing a mob execution. When the crowd dispersed, He said to her, *"Woman, where are your accusers? Has no one condemned you?"*

She said, "No man, Lord."

*And Jesus said to her, "Neither do I condemn you: go on now, and sin no more."*9

He says, *"Sin no more,"* but are you forgiven on that condition? No. When you stumble, Heaven does not revoke immunity and reinstate charges. One of the Devil's favorite tricks is to get you to beat yourself up when you fall rather than let your Abba pick you up and dust you off. That old snake wants you to hide like Adam and Eve – feeling dirty, ashamed and exposed.10 God wants you to come running into His arms of mercy. *The Fear of the Lord is Clean.*11 It does not come from shame or the dread of punishment; it comes from a love that leaves us awe-struck: a fearfully wonderful love.

The penitent Psalmist sings, *"There is forgiveness with You, that You may be feared."*12 Don't let Satan fool you. Christ, who is both your judge and your defense attorney,13 forever overturned all indictments against you.

You do not have to be good enough to be forgiven, or maintain a good record to keep in his favor. No one deserves forgiveness. If worthy of it, you would not need it. You cannot earn God's kindness, or retain it by good behavior. He grants pardon without the precondition that you do something else. He forgives you, not because you turn from evil, but because you turn to Him who delivers you from evil. He who delivers you is forming in you this same out and out mercy that you now witness in Him.

He Forgives Triumphantly

Back in the Garden of Eden, God told that slithering snake, Satan *the accuser,* that He was sending a man to crush that pointy little head.14 Jesus the Christ is that promised one whose forgiveness pounds your accuser into the blood-soaked ground of Calvary. The Old Liar's mud muffled recriminations are lost in your Lord's roar of triumph. Then turning His compassion upon you, God treads your wrong doings under foot.

The Holy Spirit gives awareness of sin to help you avoid it, not to shame you into avoiding God. Jesus did not carry your sin just to have you hide from Him. He longs for your fellowship. This conviction of sin is a winsome grace that comes by Jesus Christ.15 It is brought to our hearts by the Spirit of God who *always causes us to triumph in Christ.*16 We know that condemnation and morbid guilt are traps set by someone else.17 Let's have no part of them. We shall, however, have a part in exercising God's triumphant forgiveness.

The Legend of Private McClarty

Private McClarty was a hard drinking, brawling, career soldier. Over the years, his superiors tried every punishment they could to make him toe the line. Time in the brig, demotions in rank, fines, and hard menial labor affected the man very little, if at all. Nothing worked. Exasperated, they called him before the disciplinary council and said, "Private McClarty, since nothing this panel has done to you seems to affect any change..."

"Oh no," thought the soldier, "here comes the dishonorable discharge."

The officer continued, "We have decided to forgive you." McClarty blinked. He blinked again. Soon he was blinking back tears. Finally he stood at attention sobbing like a sad little boy. It is reported that he became an exemplary soldier.

If an institutional pardon can change a life, what can the forgiveness of God do in the lives of your obstinate acquaintances? God's forgiveness is transformative. He may plan to change people by His mercy shining through you.

He Forgives Joyously

God holds no grudges. He is not stingy with His love, hesitant with His mercy, or reluctant to absolve your guilt. He lavishes love upon you with complete, absolute, wholehearted abandon. He has no regrets or second thoughts about forgiving you. It is not like He suffered and died to pay your debt, and now He's angry about it. Rather, says the writer of Hebrews, *"For the **joy** set before him, He endured the cross and made light of the shame."*18

What was *the joy set before Him*? It was you. You are the joy set before Him. A vision of you, washed from sin and secure in the arms of your heavenly Father, made Him count the shame of the cross as a trifle. Eager to get on with an eternity of your friendship, He rose from the dead. Now He is ready to make the act of forgiving a joy for you too. Sound impossible? Let's see how He works this out...

[1]Psalms 32:1; [2]Habakkuk 1:13; [3]John 1:29; [4]Isaiah 43:25; [5]Psalm103:12; [6]Keck Observatory in Hawaii; [7]Psalm 86:5; [8]The Hard Road– J Quill; [9]John 8:3-11; [10]Genesis 3:8; [11]Psalm19:9; [12]Psalm130:4; [13]2Timothy 4:1,1John 2:1; [14]Revelation 12:10 & Genesis 3:15; [15]John 1:17, [16]1Corinthians15:57, 2Corinthians 2:14; [17]2Corinthians 2:11; [18]Hebrews 12:2

Jeff Quill

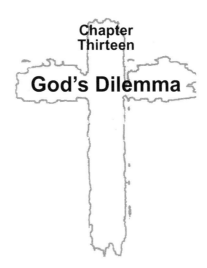

**Chapter
Thirteen**

God's Dilemma

God faces a dilemma: in The Sermon on the Mount, Jesus teaches us to pray, *"Forgive us our debts as we forgive our debtors."*1 God wants to forgive me, but if God answers that prayer, He has to forgive imperfectly like I do or not at all. Either way, it doesn't look good for me.

With this prayer, Jesus also puts me in a dilemma. I do not want to be forgiven as I forgive. I want to be forgiven the way God forgives: perfectly, eternally and absolutely. I want my sins separated from me as far as the east is from the west, and eternally forgotten. I want to obtain perfect mercy, and I want to show that same mercy.

Jesus goes on to say, *"For if you forgive men their trespasses, your heavenly Father will also forgive you: But if you forgive not men trespasses, neither will your Father forgive your trespasses."*2

The Law That Breaks Us

This troubling ultimatum is the Lord's hyper-law. By this discourse, He is upsetting any hope of successfully keeping the law, teaching it all out of our reach. We imagine ourselves up to the challenge. For that reason, Jesus magnifies its meaning. He asserts that senseless anger is murder; an insult is a path to hellfire, and lustful gazing is adultery.3 In essence; the slightest off thought or irrational tantrum is an abomination. With that dark Jewish humor, Jesus holds forth a hope; He suggests, *"You could always pluck out your eye if it wanders, or cut off your arm if it offends."*4 The point is, of course, eventually you will run out of body parts. Attempting to align ourselves with the law's demands, we find that the body and the soul are both out of line with God.

*I know that in me (that is, in my flesh) dwells no good thing.*5

The sermon is beautiful, and right, and utterly beyond our capacity to conform. To paraphrase Paul, *"The law is good, but I am not."*6 You have heard the proverb, "Rules are made to be broken."7 That is not exactly true. Rules are made to break us of thinking that we can keep the rules unbroken.

Forbidden Fruit

My friend Eugene Davis had a sweet tooth. Around Easter he knew that the orphanage supply room was a treasure trove of chocolate. The good Sisters eventually caught on to the disappearing treats. They waited in the shadows, and caught Eugene sticky handed. Sister Patrice had a great idea for discipline. She sat the boy on a wooden chair, and stacked boxes of chocolate bunnies all around him. "Eat." she commanded. Eugene began to devour the sweets with great enthusiasm. The chair was located at the front end of a room containing about fifty metal-framed beds lined in five rows. The nun's cubical occupied the front corner of the dorm. Built so that she could always hear what was going on in the bed rows, its green wainscoted walls stood ten feet high under the fifteen-foot ceiling.

The thief sat in the dark nibbling away at his punishment while the rest of us, filled with envy, lay in our beds.

"Pssst. Eugene, Gimme one."

"Me too. Eugene."

"Eugene."

"Hey Eugene, over here...."

Sister Patrice called from behind her wall, "I hear you out there. If you want to end up like Mr. Davis, you just go right ahead and join him."

Mayhem. Sheets and pillows flew off as though a mighty wind blew through the hall. The room thundered as a hundred bare feet pounded the wooden floor. We rushed the chocolate stash with shouts and squeals of joy. The nun hopped out of bed stumbling and fumbling for her robe. She came running out swinging her flannel belt; driving us frenzied animals back to our beds. Eugene continued his lonely, miserable vigil late into the night until he was very sick. The next Easter, he was caught stealing chocolates again. The law looks so deliciously do-able. The Lord really stacks it high before we figure out we don't have the stomach for it.

The Law Of The Lord Is Perfect 8

The law-tangled, rule-happy Galatians were told, *"All the law is fulfilled in this one statement: Love your neighbor as yourself."*9

This is the whole of it. Practically everyone agrees that this is a beautiful law. It's worth the effort. If you can just do this perfectly, remembering that this love includes all the other rules, you'll have everything worked out. But I jest. We know that no one but Christ Jesus fulfills this law. No one. The original Mosaic injunction was two sided: one side prohibits getting even or holding grudges, the other side mandates love instead: *Do not take revenge or bear a grudge against the children of your people, but you shall love your neighbor as yourself; I am the Lord.*10

God tells us from the beginning that love is inextricably tied to forgiveness. As long as we are sinners living among sinners, love will mean forgiveness. If I could love my neighbor as myself, I could forgive my neighbor as myself. But Jesus adds this stipulation, *"Be perfect as your Father in heaven is perfect."*11 Do any of us really think we can live up to this demand? Forgive with perfect forgiveness? Forgiveness that is less than His, will always be flawed and thus inadequate before God. If we could keep the whole of God's Law without a scratch, we could claim some sufficiency, but no one will ever, ever keep it intact and unbent. That is our predicament. It is an impossible quandary. Happily for us, our heavenly Father takes joy in doing the impossible.

Christ presses this law, this injunction to forgive flawlessly, not to be mean, but to bring us to this frame of mind: *"God be merciful to me a sinner."*[12] Heaven's teacher amplifies the dilemma for which He is the only solution. He uses The Lord's Prayer as our schoolmaster to bring us unto Himself.[13] The lesson He wants us to learn is: *"Without me ye can do nothing."*[14]

By divine coincidence, the middle verse of the whole Bible is Psalm118:8, which says, *"It is better to trust in the LORD than to put confidence in man."* That verse also belongs in the middle of our hearts and minds. It is better to put our faith in Christ than believe in ourselves to do these things.

Faith

The Bible concludes that, *a man is made right by faith – without the deeds of the law.*[15] Made right without the Law? That is very good news. It gives me hope. Where can I get this faith; where does it come from; how can I obtain it?

There are different kinds of faith. Some athletes imagine a performance for hours, trying to believe their way to excellence. Attempting to believe his way to financial success, a businessman repeats affirmations about wealth. A man may chant into euphoria, trying simply to believe in a deity, even if that happens to be himself. Oddly enough, religious belief is often mere **intellectual acquiescence** to a system of dogmas, rituals, or an organized system of superstitions. Some espouse a sort of myths-to-live-by methodology. All these are typical functions of the human mind. But the faith the Bible speaks of is not a natural ability or faculty of concentration. It is from another source.

Look at the faith that lives in you, Christian. You know that you believe some extraordinary things. You believe that God became a man. You believe He walked on water, healed the sick, gave sight to the blind, raised the dead, died for you, and then got up from the dead, and ascended into Heaven. More astounding still, you believe that there are three persons in one God. There is no denying you possess a marvelous faith.

Here is a very important scripture verse – *By grace are you saved through faith; and that not of yourselves: that faith is the gift of God.*[16] God gave you that amazing faith by His amazing grace. It is, in fact, the faith of Jesus Christ Himself. As Paul declares, *"I live by the faith of the Son of God."*[17] More than a mere faith **in** the Son, it is a faith **of** the Son.

Here is how this faith comes to us, how God deals to every person a measure of this faith.[18] When we were unbelieving, we heard the gospel, or it came to mind, or a breathtakingly beautiful starry night sky declared the glory of God to us.[19] Hearing the story, we found in our hearts a desire to believe. We knew we could believe if we chose to, because the capacity to do so was right there on our hearts like morning dew on roses.[20]

The Spirit of the Son visited your heart, touching it with His faith so that you know that you know that you know. In the same way, He touched you with His forgiveness. The Faith and Love you find dwelling in you right now came by the clear, intimate whispers[21] of the Son of God. His forgiveness already lives in you just as sure as His faith lives in you. It is God's key to the ingenious resolution of His dilemma...

[1]Matthew 6:12; [2]Matthew 6:14; [3]Matthew 5:21-22,28; [4]Matthew 5:29,30; [5]Romans 7:18; [6]Romans7:14, [7]D.McArthur; [8]Psalm 19:7; [9]Galatians 5:14; [10]Leviticus 19:18; [11]Matthew5:48; [12]Luke18:1-3; [13]Galatians 3:24; [14]John 15:5; [15]Romans 3:28; [16]Ephesians 2:8; [17]Galatians; 2:20(Some translate this "IN the Son" but "OF the Son" is a correct rendering.); [18]Romans 12:3; [19]Psalm 19:1; [20]Hosea 14:5; [21]1Kings 19:12

**Chapter
Fourteen**

The Fix

Look here now, I stand at the door, and knock if any man hear my voice, and open the door, I will come in to him, *and will sup with him, and he with me.* Revelation 3:20

I remember when, as a young man aspiring to atheism, I stood on the front porch one troubled night. My thoughts turned to the question of God, and a deep peace overtook me. I was swept away with it for one swooning moment. My anxiety settled, and I sensed a sweet, pungent inner peace. I shook loose and recited my silly mantra, "God is an excuse for man's ignorance," then scurried back into the house to escape the God who was not out there on the porch. The Holy Spirit persistently tugs on the heart. Many of us shrug it off again and again until at last we give in to it and discover to our delight the presence of Christ.

The Voice of God

Our faith is the evidence of things not seen.[1] It is the proof that God silently shouts[2] the Word into us, speaking this faith into our hearts just as He spoke the world around us into existence.

Faith comes by hearing, and the hearing comes from the living word breathed into our souls by God.[3] The attraction to God we sensed in the midst of our unbelief was the Christ standing so close to us we could feel His faith on our souls. By the love of the Holy Spirit, He breathes His faith into our hearts causing us to hope, and initiating that trust we find within us when we hear the Word of God.4

When Jesus rose from the dead, He worked a surprise on a couple of His friends. They were hiking home when He walked up and joined them. Constraining their eyes so that they could not recognize Him, He said, "*You look so sad; what are you talking about?*" They told Him all about Himself, His death and the disturbing fact that some women claimed He was alive. Jesus explained things to them as they walked along. Once home, they recognized Him and He vanished from sight.

*They said to one another, "Did not our heart burn within us, while He talked with us on the way here, and opened the scriptures to us."*5

When the Spirit spoke to you, you may not have recognized Him, but your heart caught fire with His faith. Most of the time, when Jesus talks to our hearts we don't recognize we are being spoken to, let alone who is speaking to us. Even Mary Magdalene, a close and dear friend of Jesus, did not recognize Him after He rose from the dead. She thought her dear friend was the gardener until He said her name.6 This encounter inspired these words from an old hymn

And He walks with me, and He talks with me
And He tells me I am His own
And the joy we share as we tarry there
None other has ever known7

You may not have realized it, but Jesus has been walking and talking with you, igniting your faith with His words. By taking that faith as your own you took Jesus Himself, for He is not separate from His faith. He gives you no gift apart from Himself. Just as He gave you His faith, so He gave you His forgiveness. He gave you His Spirit and all His virtues; all His righteousnesses. All this is now in you, awaiting expression; awaiting release. Think of a seed ready to sprout, and you have a picture of God's love growing from your heart. Think of a chick breaking it's shell, and you have a picture of God's love breaking through into your world.

Our Source

Look again at what Paul said of this Faith. *"I live by faith of the Son of God."*[8] He says, *"I **live** by Faith,"* because the word *"**Live**"* encompasses everything, including forgiveness: the particular aspect of God's life we are discussing. If we paraphrase this verse to address our topic of concern, we have: "I forgive by faith of the Son of God who loved me and gave himself for me."

Knowing the source of the Christian's virtue, the source of the Christian's righteousness and in particular, the Christian's ability to forgive, helps us exercise forgiveness. The foundation is not will power, positive thinking, or obedience to the law. The forgiveness based on these things is as weak as we are. Early on we learned that little pigs who build walls of such twigs and straw soon have no houses at all. We must look elsewhere.

To begin with, God gives us the faith, and then counts that faith as a righteousness not our own. Just as *Abraham believed God, and it was credited to him as righteousness,*[9] so also the Father sees us as righteous. It is because He sees the faith of Christ living in us. God sees His only begotten Son believing through our awakened hearts. The faith that is the gift from God is counted as righteousness, because that is just what it **is.**

You are sitting at the dinner table, and you see peaches in an old cracked bowl at the other end. You don't say, "Pass me that cracked bowl." You say, "Please pass those peaches." When God looks in your direction, He sees not a cracked pot, but a peach. He sees not a doubting sinner, but the faithful Christ.

Our Righteousness

Paul says that Jesus Christ is *"made unto us Righteousness."*[10] The prophets call Him, *"The lord our righteousness."*[11] If something good is coming from us, it is coming from the Spirit of Christ in us. In the end, righteousness is love. He is our righteousness (our love) and therefore, He is our ability to forgive. Where we fall down, He stands up for us. Where we fail, He succeeds. He gives Himself to be our love. By virtue of His life in our hearts, His heart of virtue is ours for life. Through Him *we are partakers of the divine nature,*[12] and as we have seen, it is in the divine nature to forgive.

Of course, it takes a while to work this out into our daily lives. It is like learning to dance with Papa. I loved dancing with my children when they were very small. Now it's my grandchildren spinning around the room in my arms. Sometimes they hold tight to Boppa's neck. Other times they lean back with arms outstretched in complete abandon, as we bob and twirl to the music. The more they trust me, the more they dance my dance. It follows that the more I trust my heavenly Father, the more I will move by His love.

Paul said, "I want *to be found in Him, not having my own righteousness based on rules, but that righteousness which comes by the faith of Christ, the righteousness from God through faith.*"13 Let's again paraphrase using the particular dance we are interested in here: to be found in Him, not having my own forgiveness based on rules, but that forgiveness which comes by the faith of Christ, the forgiveness from God through faith. The whole Christian life, from the first "Yes Lord," to the last "I come," is by this faith. We forgive...by faith and *that not of ourselves, it is the gift of God.*14

The Unraveled Dilemma

Instead of coming down to our level of stingy charity, He raises us up to His level of lavish mercy. He provides us with His love by which we can forgive. Since He alone is perfect, the only way to answer the dilemma of the Lord's Prayer is to cause us to act as He acts. By endowing us with His forgiving heart, He enables us to forgive with His perfect forgiveness.

Cracks in the Fellowship

In resolving the second half of the dilemma stated in: *"If you forgive not men their trespasses neither will your Father forgive you,"* parents all over the world tell their kids, "If you won't eat your peas you can just go hungry." If I don't forgive, I can just go without. Remember, Christ is my only forgiveness. There is not one mercy I receive for myself, and another I give to you. The forgiveness I withhold from you is also meant for me. We are all in the same boat. Chopping a hole in your hull just sinks my canoe. The unforgiveness that breaks my fellowship with you breaks my fellowship with God. If I push forgiveness away, I push my Father away. He does not like to be pushed. The sweet communion between Father and child is interrupted. A condition He does not abide for long. Too deep is His love for me. His woodshed swiftly remedies that situation. So I have noticed.

Christ is made unto us the righteousness that is perfect love. He is made unto us the perfect love that is forgiveness. And while this does not yet show us **how** to forgive, it does show us who our forgiveness is and where it comes from. The forgiveness we seek to employ is Jesus Christ Himself.

Our faith is not an idea; it is a person. Our forgiveness is not some high ideal; it is The Most High God. Our love is not just a superb notion; it is the Supreme Being. This is far more than a way of life; it is *The Way the truth and the Life.*[15]

How shall this Life live out?...

[1]Hebrews 11:1; [2]Kings 19:12; [3]Romans 10:17; [4]Psalm 119:49 & Psalm 22:9; [5]Luke 24:13-32; [6]John 20:15; [7]In The Garden –Miles; [8]Galatians 2:20; [9]Romans 4:3; [10]1Corinthians 1:30; [11]Jeremiah 33:16; [12]2 Peter1:4; [13]Philippians3:9; [14]Ephesians2:8; [15]John 14:6

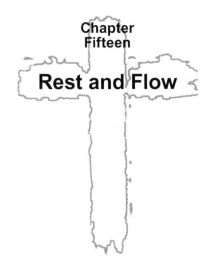

Chapter Fifteen

Rest and Flow

What is our part in this? That becomes more evident as we rest in God like a little child cuddled on the lap of mama or papa. A child in the arms of a loving parent perfectly illustrates the rest and security God wants for us. Oblivious to the cares of the world, the youngster lays her head just under her papa's chin, where she hears his heartbeat and feels his breath on the top of her head. This is the intimacy that makes everything all right. Task number one is learning to rest in Him.

He who has entered into God's rest has also ceased from his own works just as God did ...(on the seventh day of creation). *Let us labor therefore to enter into that rest.*[1] This is the hard and frightening work of Christianity: dropping all control and casting all care into the hands of God.

Jesus says, *"Come unto me all you who labor and are weighed down and I will give you rest."*[2] He calls us to drop the weight of obligation and conformity, cease from our laborious piety, and let Him do the heavy lifting of the spiritual life. Though counter intuitive, you can be confident of precisely this thing: *that He who has begun a good work in you will perform it until the day of Jesus Christ.*[3]

The Work of Rest

Here is how Jesus said it works. We rest as we labor. He compares us to beasts of burden: oxen, horses, mules, or the like. Not such a big stretch. He invites us, *"Take my yoke upon you, and learn of me; for I am meek and lowly in heart: and you shall find rest unto your souls. For my yoke is easy, and my burden is light."*[4] As an inner city boy, the first time I heard this I thought it was a quote from a poem. I assumed that *yolk* meant "egg yolk." Obviously some obscure symbolism. Deep. For my equally befuddled fellow urbanites: A yoke is a device for hooking a wagon or plow to work animals. It fits around the animal's head, shoulders and chest, and then attaches to whatever someone wants moved. The ox leans his weight into the yoke, resting in it as he moves forward. Now, instead of some ox leaning on a wooden frame, imagine yourself leaning on the invisible arms of God, falling forward onto the arms that built the universe.

O how sweet to walk in this pilgrim way,

Leaning on the everlasting arms;

O how bright the path grows from day to day,

Leaning on the everlasting arms.[5]

Legend has it that people came from all over Israel to the Bar-Yosef Wood-shop, because Joseph and Jesus carved the easiest fitting yokes in the country. We lean into the support cut just for us by the carpenter who promises the burden will be light – He already carries it. He also carries us. *I have made and I will carry you*[6]

As we rest and move, so we rest and flow. Soon we shall discuss how to know it is His work of forgiveness and not ours. Let it suffice for now to say, the rest he calls us to is not a dead stop, it is a gentle, unseen flow like sap in a vine. Jesus compares the love of God to the sap that flows through the vine – to the branches – and into the fruit saying, *"As the branch cannot bear fruit of itself, except it lives on the vine; no more can you, except you live in me. I am the vine, you are the branches: He that dwells in me, and I in him, the same bears a lot of fruit: for without me you can do nothing."*[7] We don't originate the life flow or create the fruit; we merely rest in Christ as a branch rests in the vine. What is in the vine naturally flows through the branch. No strain, just rest in the connection. The more we rely on, live in, and attend to that bond, the stronger the flow.

Spending Time

It is a simple matter of taking time to enjoy your Heavenly Papa. Taking pleasure in His companionship, telling Him all about your day, your thoughts, hopes and frustrations; praising Him, or maybe saying nothing at all – just being with Him. In quiet communion with God, the Holy Spirit can clear our vision. Sometimes we think we are upset with a person, when actually we are just disappointed with the way things worked out. Often, God will reveal this, and show us what is really troubling us.

The flesh always looks for someone to blame, even when no one is at fault. It's just tough living in this world. Like my grandson said in a note he wrote to me, "Lif is HorD. so is schooL." The Spirit is called *The Comforter*, [9] and spending time with Him is a salve for the everyday abrasions, bumps, and bruises that come with living and learning.

Every week I advised my young students, "Don't forget to take your walks with the Lord." I think it is no coincidence that God uses the word "walk," when describing your life with Him. One prophet says that the Lord's pleasure is having you *walk humbly with your God.*[8] It may primarily be a figure of speech, but God drops a not-too-subtle hint here. Your Father loves visiting with you.

The story is told of a little girl's explanation of the verse, *"Enoch walked with God, and vanished because God took him away."*[10]

She said, "Enoch and God were good friends. They loved to take long walks together every day, and then return to Enoch's house. One day they were on an extra long walk and God said, 'Since we're closer to My house now than to your house, why don't you come home with Me today?' Enoch liked it there so much, he just never came back."

I love what the Wstminster Catechism says:

Question: What is the chief end of man?

Answer: Man's chief end is to glorify God, and to enjoy him forever.

According to Jesus, *"This is what glorifies your Father – you producing bunches of fruit."*[11] He is glorified as you delight in Him and so let His love flow out through your life. *Delight yourself in the LORD; and He shall...bring out your righteousness as the streaming light of dawn.* [12]

Rivers, Dams and Jams

God's forgiveness comes to us like a free-flowing river. Our personal brand of righteousness obstructs it. That is why Jesus said, *"If you forgive not men their trespasses, neither will your Father forgive your trespasses,"*[13] In words that fit our metaphor, "If you damn the river, your heavenly Father will have to stop the flow." Every stream has a bed on which it rests and flows; forgiveness rests and flows on our fellowship with Christ. Our futile, self-reliant labor blocks the current. It stops the stream that is forgiveness.

In the early twentieth century northwestern United States, logjams occurred when timber floated down river to the mills. Where the river was narrow or obstructed by rocks, log drivers known as "River Pigs," loosed jams that were over twenty feet high. They waded through ice flows from dawn to dark. If a man slipped and dropped through the massive, bobbing, twisting log fields, his body might never resurface.

The image is a good allegory for the pardon of God. Like the lumberjacks, He sends His mercy through our hearts out to those in our stream of contact. The flow ceases if something comes up to block His kindness. Our offended sense of justice, our righteous indignation or – more likely – our lack of fellowship with our loving Heavenly Father jams up the log booms. No forgiveness going out, means no forgiveness coming in. What caused the backup? The old critter. Unlike the easygoing otter floating downstream resting on his back, we favor the busy beaver. Constructing fat dams, we drop big self-virtuous timbers across the channel. The trouble is – this old unforgiving inner varmint. We tangle. *For what our old sin nature lusts after is contrary to what the Spirit wills, and what the Spirit wants is opposed to our human nature.*[14]

We are going to go round and round with this fallen nature for as long as we live. The old flesh will always resist the Divine Love, stubbornly refusing to let the Spirit through. Our God will outlast it; He shall see to it that we defeat the little beast. Contrary to our old nature, the motion of God's love is going to bring us to give way, rest and forgive.

*He will rest you in His Love.*15

Count on it, as sure as He is living and the tide will rise, He is going to free us up and move His love downstream.

As in the beginning, *the Spirit moved upon the face of the waters,*16 so it is now. If it cannot move, it is not the Spirit. God's flowing love teems with life; bad blood stagnates. The motion of the Spirit in our hearts carries forgiveness from God to those who offend us. Forgiveness is free-flowing love, not an isolated incident like a sand-spit on the river. The gift in us, far from inert and static, is alive and powerful. Hardly a rigid memorial to the Lord, it is a vibrant, frolicking tribute to His love.

*But whosoever drinks of the water that I shall give him shall never thirst; but the water that I shall give him shall be in him a fountain spring of water gushing everlasting life. He who believes in Me, as the Scripture said, From his deep inner being will flow torrents of living water.*17 What stops His movement, also stops His forgiveness, but not for long. Heaven's River Pig works the narrow channels of our hearts. If something is stuck in our soul, He will loosen it by and by. God did not sacrifice His own Son only to allow a little psychological jam to halt the motion of His love. *Because the love of God floods our hearts, by the Holy Spirit who is given to us.*18

We are now ready to see how we can begin to open the floodgates...

1Hebrews 4:11; 2Matthew11:28; 3Philippians1:6; 4Matthew11:29,30; 5Leaning On The Everlasting Arms-Hoffman; 6Isaiah 46:4; 7John15:4-5; 8Micah6:8; 9John14:16; 10Genesis 5:24; 11John 15:8; 12Psalm 37:4; 13Matthew6:15; 14Galatians5:17; 15Zephaniah 3:17; 16Genesis 1:2; 17John 4:14, 7:38; 18Romans 5:5.

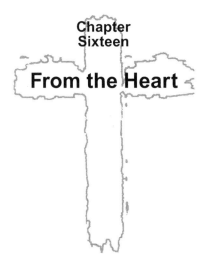

Chapter Sixteen

From the Heart

The kingdom of heaven is like unto leaven, which a woman took, and hid in three measures of meal, till the whole was leavened. Matthew 13:33

The Torah required the Jews to remove all yeast from their houses during Passover. This week long observation was also called the Feast of Unleavened Bread, which we know as matzo bread made from just flour, water and a pinch of salt. For homemakers, the purge was simply inconvenient. So one young mother, we'll call her Rachel, came up with the brilliant idea that she would hide the yeast somewhere in the house.

"That way I won't have to go out and buy new yeast next week. But where can I put it? Ah! No one will ever suspect the flour jar." She pushed the moist lump of yeast down into the flour, and feeling quite clever, went about her merry way. When it came time to make the matzo, she scooped up some flour, made the paste, rolled it flat, and set it in the sun to bake.

Later, when she came out to check on the cakes, she found the neighbors gathered around the platter smiling and chuckling. The leavened cakes had risen in the hot sun to fine round loaves. The Rabbi, stroking his beard, said as solemnly as he could, "Well, Rachel, at least the yeast is not in the house."

This embellished version of the story Jesus told shows how the kingdom of heaven works in us. Like yeast in flour, when God's love enters our hearts it grows and changes us. It is *alive and active*[1] even though we may not notice it. The love that hides in us is Christ Himself, and so it rises. (Pun intended.) *We have this treasure in clay jars, that the immeasurable excellence of this power may be this: God, and none of us.*[2]

To take the Lord's forgiveness to heart is to take the Lord to heart. Receiving His forgiveness is also receiving Him. This forgiveness is Jesus Christ Himself – the perfect love we are discovering within our imperfect selves.

She, therefore, who has Jesus in her heart, has forgiveness in her heart. He, therefore, who has Jesus in his heart, has forgiveness in his heart. Whoever, therefore, has Jesus within has forgiveness within.

Knowing this, let's open some simple, elementary ways to exercise that forgiveness.

An Exercise

Like a newborn colt trying out its legs, this little exercise will help get our feet under us. It's a couple of things I practice when I feel something is impossible to forgive. This is just a beginning, a sort of stop gap measure between fledgling inability and mature capability, but it can help when we feel that no one can reasonably be expected to forgive a certain offence.

When some one who did me wrong comes to mind, I will refer to that person as "Mr. or Mrs. So-And-So, The Forgiven." I can say this because Christ has indeed purchased their pardon. I tell the absent offender, "You are forgiven from my heart. Christ forgives you from my heart." The declaration of forgiveness, though it seems to contradict my experience, is nonetheless true, because Christ himself has forgiven from His place in my heart as much as from His throne in heaven. Jesus not only forgives my sins, but also the sins of those who have done me wrong. I have faith in His forgiveness, and so do you. We claim this forgiveness as our own – the forgiveness we hold up to God is His own.

Paul said, *"I live, yet not I, but Christ lives in me. And what I now live in the flesh I live by faith of the Son of God."*[3]

Again, he says, "*I **live**,*" because the word, *"**live**"* encompasses everything we do: I forgive, yet not I, but Christ forgives in me. And what I now forgive in the flesh I forgive by faith of the Son of God."

Jesus said, *"Forgive from your hearts."*4 Christ is the "heart of my own heart."5 He forever lives more myself than I myself. As we crack open the door of forgiveness, this exercise will do as – **from** the heart. When the door is fully opened we shall see how to forgive **with** the heart.

Feelings

The forgiveness is from our hearts. We may not always feel it, but it is no less so. Feelings are like dessert: they are delicious but not at all necessary to a good meal. Nevertheless, the Lord knows we need to feel good. As with any necessity, Jesus tells us, *"your Heavenly Abba knows you have need of all these things."*6 But through this next verse, God cautions us about elevating our moods artificially. *"Be not drunk with wine but be filled with the Spirit."*7 Substance abuse makes it harder to forgive and forget the pain. Take it from someone who knows: the temptation is promising, but the reward less than inadequate – it is malignant and destructive. The serenity and contentment we need are incidental to our union with Christ. Because of our oneness with Him, we begin by and by to share His tranquility, our pain subsides, and our good humor returns. *The fruit of the Spirit is love: joy, and peace* 8… Christ your joy, who *will never leave you, nor forsake you,*9 is always present though not always felt. He gives a spiritual joy that goes deeper than soul, deeper than your senses. The apostle demonstrates this paradox when he describes himself *"As sorrowful, yet always rejoicing."*10

The acrid feelings change by and by, and often instantly. We don't understand how He works it in us, but He does. No matter how we feel, He forgives our adversaries from our innermost being. Keeping with the images offered by Paul and Jesus: God forgives from within these *"earthenware jars of leavened flour."* By Faith in Jesus Christ we declare to our offenders, "You are forgiven from my heart." The forgiver is the Spirit of Christ. While forgiveness seems out of reach, He will take our part until we learn to partake of His divine nature; for soon we shall forgive with a *demonstration of the Spirit and power.*[11] He is our capacity to forgive. It is He we learn to extend to others.

Satan the accuser, seething over the Lord's coup d'état, may snivel, "Why that's unfair. It is not really you. It is *the just for the unjust.*"[12]

"So it is," we answer, "but it is a perfect forgiveness coming from our hearts. And it must chafe being you."

The mercy sent into your heart by His Spirit is yours for the giving. Forgiveness that comes to you from God is the same forgiveness by which you forgive. The same wonderful grace with which you are forgiven is the grace with which you forgive. Not yours. His. He who took your place on the cross takes your place in life. Christ in heaven, who forgave your debts, is the Christ in your heart who forgives your debtors.

The gate is open. While this does show that God covers for us when we cannot see our way clear to forgive, it does not yet show us how we forgive. So let's read on…

[1]Hebrews 4:12; [2]2Corinthians 4:7; [3]Gal 2:20; [4]Matthew 6:15; [5]Be Thou My Vision–Hull & Byrne; [6]Matthew 6:32; [7]Ephesians5:18; [8]Galatians 5:22; [9]Hebrews 12:11; [10]2Corinthians6:10; [11]1Corinthians 2:4; [12]1Peter 3:18

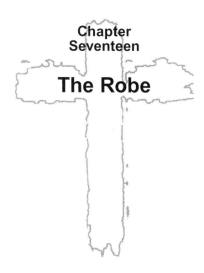

**Chapter
Seventeen**

The Robe

*Now Israel loved Joseph more than all his children, because he
was the son of his old age: and he made him a coat of many
colors.* Genesis 37:3

Sometimes your Heavenly Father's love can make you
feel like you are His favorite child. That's just the way His love
is. Like Jacob favoring his son Joseph, God gives you a coat of
many colors: the Spirit of Christ covers you like a beautiful over-
coat. Scripture puts it this way: *"Let us walk…not in strife…but
put on the Lord Jesus Christ."*1

Here the Christ is compared to clothing in which we con-
sciously dress ourselves. We wear Him like a robe, and walk
around like Him in this world. To Isaiah it was like wedding ap-
parel; he called them *"the clothes of salvation"* and *"the robe of
righteousness."* God dresses you with a garment of glory2 for the
royal ball – the celebration of forgiveness.

This is something I practice. I acknowledge that I am in
Christ, dwelling in His person, enveloped head to toe in His invisible glory as in a garment of holy light. It is a very effective escape
from temptation.

Putting on Christ means two things: we are wrapped in Him – enfolded in His being – it also means we cloak our actions in the imitation of Jesus.

First, About the Outfit:

This is not some mere mental exercise or some creative fantasy. It is not pretense. This next verse makes it clear that we, in spiritual reality, wear Christ, *"For as many of you as were baptized into Christ have put on Christ."*3 We acknowledge this truth; we do not create it. The old masters used to depict this as a halo. In religious pictures they painted a globe of light around a saint's head. What is a saint, really? A teacher of mine used to say, "A saint is a sinner whose sins ain't: it's a forgiven sinner, one whose sins are covered by Christ."4 That is a description of you, believer; you are a saint by faith in Jesus, covered, clothed, and surrounded by the invisible Light. You have put on Christ.

Secondly, About the *"Put On"*:

The other meaning is: Once dressed, we put on an act – His act – particularly His act of forgiveness. We just start acting like what He says we are in Him.

*Put on therefore…the gut level core of mercies…forgiving one another even as Christ forgave you.*5 In this passage the apostle clearly identifies the Christ-robe as the heart of forgiveness. Because Christ is our forgiveness we *put on* His mercy, we **dress up** in His kindness. We suit-up on the inside, and act the way He does. As we move like Him, He moves with us, in us, and through us. We face the direction He travels, and He carries us in His power.

*Put off the old self…and put on the new self, which, in the likeness of God, was created in… holy kindness.*6 We *"put on"* a display of the kindness Christ is in us. This is not a show for the world, but a form for God to fill. Because He is in us, and we are in Him, we can do this. We just need to lean and step in the direction God is moving. You see, the Spirit of God's forgiveness moves through us; since that is our source, we need to face in the direction He is going. We put up the sails of imitation that the Spirit-Wind7 fills with holy kindness. The sails appear empty, but we believe in a God *who calls those things which be not as though they were.*8

Christ in Action

Let's look now to the Gospel of Luke and watch Christ as He forgives. We'll see how we can act as He does, that is, put Him on; dress from His wardrobe, especially His coat of forgiveness. To imitate the forgiving Christ, we look to Calvary where our Savior calls to our Father from the cross, *"Father, forgive them; for they know not what they do."*[9]

This prayer is something we can emulate. We can put the forgiveness of God into action by asking – simply asking God to forgive those who have hurt us. Since the forgiveness God calls for takes a love impossibly greater than ours, we do as Christ did: we call on our Father to do it. Finding our charity inadequate, we ask our Father to absolve our foes. Jesus did this, and His forgiveness was perfect. It makes sense then for those of us who are somewhat less than perfect. We first ask God to forgive them because in the end it is God who forgives through us. He is *the Alpha and the Omega, the Beginning and the End* of our forgiveness. [10]

In the parable of the unforgiving servant, the creditor-king thought that the servant forgiven so much ought to also show mercy. He assumed that a man shown compassion would naturally show compassion. But the story lays bare the fact that it does not always work out that way. People do not usually forgive just because they are forgiven. We are told to "forgive even as Christ forgave you,"[5] and Christ did not forgive us because He was forgiven. He forgave us by the same love that He has now planted in our hearts. When we say, "Father forgive them," It is **His** prayer, by **His** love, and **His** Spirit, not ours. Even when we don't know what to say, *the Spirit braces our feeble souls...the Spirit itself intercedes for us with deep sighs that cannot be expressed in words.*[11] We but come to the Father and present our hearts.

As I lay in an Albuquerque hospital nursing a bad case of frostbite, orderlies brought an unconscious young man in to share the room. He was in rough shape; the victim of an assault. It was a day or two before we could talk. When he could finally speak, he told me of the painful betrayal that lead to a severe beating. Then he said something I found odd, "Señor Jeff, I pray God will forgive them. They have done a very bad thing. I just hope God will forgive them." I didn't say it to him at the time, but I thought, "Why don't **you** just forgive them yourself?" But now I can see the wisdom in what my fellow patient was saying. The wounds were too fresh, and he did not fool himself into thinking he could forgive in his own power. Like his Master, in his time of trial he called on God to forgive, leaning not to his own forgiveness, but trusting in the Lord with all his heart.12

Saul and Steven

This is how, in the early days of the church, Deacon Steven did it. When a mob *drove him out of the city, and stoned him. Witnesses laid down their clothes at the feet of one Saul of Tarsus who was overseeing the execution. They stoned Stephen as he kneeled down, and cried with a loud voice, "Lord, do not lay this sin to their charge." When he had said this, he fell asleep.*13

Did God answer this prayer? Let us see. Saul of Tarsus becomes Paul the Apostle and writes, *"I am the least of the apostles, not fit to be called an apostle, because I persecuted the church of God. But by the grace of God I am what I am: and His grace to me was not in vain; but I worked ever so much harder than all the other apostles: yet not I, but the grace of God which was with me."*14

I have quoted much of the work of Paul, because he knew like few others, what it is to be forgiven, and what it is to forgive. He labored lovingly because, to him, so much was forgiven. Note also that he understood that the labor was not of him, but of that grace that attends us. It all comes from having friends who wear the right coat: calling for God's forgiveness instead of their own.

When we speak if Jesus in heaven, we usually say, *"He is seated at the right hand of the Father."*15 Before he passed on, Steven saw Jesus, not seated, but standing at the right hand of the Father.16 The Savior stood to honor the deacon's imminent call for forgiveness. When we ask God to forgive, we draw His applause. Who knows but that the soul we thus forgive may someday, like Paul, change the world through Christ.

Invoking God's forgiveness then, brings us closer to full participation in His love. As we move to do what God is doing, He will do it through us. Because it is His virtue at work in us, we shape our actions to look like His actions.

This takes us a step further into God's forgiveness. There is much more. We see that Christ forgives for us and through us; now let's see **how we** forgive through Him. We are ready to travel deep into the Father's heart...

Romans 13:13-14; 2Isaiah 61:10, Isaiah 61:3; 3Galatians 3:27; 4BG Leonard; 5Colossians 3:12; 6Ephesians 4:24; 7Acts 2:2; 8Romans 4:17; 9Luke 23:34; 10Revelation 1:8; 11Romans 8:26; 12Proverbs 3:5; 13Acts 7:58-60; 141Corinthians 15:9,10; 15Hebrews 12:2; 16Acts 7:56

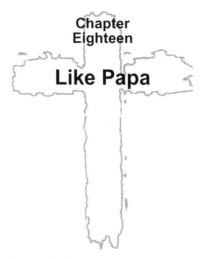

Chapter Eighteen

Like Papa

This is the way, walk ye in it. Isaiah 30:21

I couldn't get to sleep – four A.M. and I was still pacing the floor. Indignation smoldered in my head, fueled by some nasty church politics. My pride stinging and my stomach knotted, I fumed over the injustice of it. At the end of myself, I asked God to help me let go of the anger. This is what He showed me.

Having a miserable time trying to pardon a betrayal, my mind turned to a petition in the Lord's Prayer: *"Forgive us our debts as we forgive our debtors."*1 I understood that the Spirit forgave my offenders from my heart, and I asked God to forgive them. Now my soul ached to fully participate in that release – to forgive as God forgives, but how was that?

"Papa, how do **You** forgive?"

Like He speaks to most of you, so with me, God voices His thoughts with no language or sound; it is a silent, wordless awareness of His truth. I'm going to try to put that night into words for you.

He said, "I forgive by the blood of the Lamb. I forgive you because My Son Jesus paid for your sin. I accept that payment for your sins. Now you too forgive because Jesus died for the sin of those who betrayed you. Accept His payment for those sins."

I asked, "I forgive by faith in the Blood of Christ?"

"Yes," He answered, "You forgive by faith in the Blood of Christ."

When what comes to mind lines up with the Word of God, and clearly this did, I know my Lord has spoken to me.

I took to my knees. In my heart I looked, not to my betrayers, but to the Christ crucified for them. I felt Him say, "Is this enough?" Shocked, humbled, and broken by the question, I answered through my sorrow and tears, "Yes, Lord. It is enough. It is enough."

The burden of resentment dropped away; its departure felt so liberating that I jumped to my feet and began to dance about the room before the Lord, singing "Holy, Holy, Holy," clapping my hands in applause of His mercy. I'll admit, I'm glad no one was around to witness that spectacle. But I couldn't help myself. Jesus set me free of that enslaving grudge. His joy flooded my heart. *If the Son therefore shall make you free, you shall be free indeed.*2 But fear not little flock, dancing, singing and clapping your hands are not necessary components of forgiving.

The Key

Jesus promised the keys of the Kingdom to those who accept His unique Christhood.3 The key to forgiving is contained in a passage broken up and sometimes lost between the artificial chapter divisions of the New Testament. This particular teaching is easily overlooked because it starts at the end of a chapter and continues into the next. At the end of one chapter, Paul exhorts us to *Be kind one to another, tender-hearted, forgiving one another, even as God for Christ's sake has forgiven you.*4 God forgave you because of what Jesus did: He forgave you **for Christ's sake**.

Continuing with that same thought on the other side of the chapter break, he encourages us to *be, therefore, imitators of God, as dear children.*5 Since God forgives for Christ's sake, you do the same. As a little child, you imitate your Papa. The passage may also be translated thus:

God, for Christ sake, has forgiven you,
therefore be imitators of this as God's dear children.

Kids love to imitate what they see their parents do. It is an important part of play. Jesus invites us to *become as little chil-*

*dren*6 so that we can enter into these things. My one-year-old grandson was fascinated by the power of keys. Whenever he came to visit he wanted Gah-pah's keys. He couldn't figure out how to work them, but he tried them on everything, even the cat. Our Father wants us to take His key and forgive the same way He does – for the sake of the Suffering Christ. We forgive because of what Jesus did on the cross. We do it just like we see Abba do it. He wants all His *dear children* to imitate Him.

Passover.

Part of our play is a re-enactment of our Papa's great *Passover* in the Land of Egypt. For centuries Egypt enslaved the children of Israel. God sent Moses to Pharaoh with the message, *"Let My people Go."*7

The ruler, considered a god in his own right, hardened his heart, disdaining the God of low-born slaves. After devastating the Egyptians with plagues, the "slave God," as Pharaoh might have called Him, prepared to *strike down all the firstborn in their land, the best of all their strength.*8 The Egyptian oppression cost every firstborn male his life.

God ordered His people to kill a lamb: an *unblemished male,* and smear the blood around the door-frames of their houses. *For I will pass through the land and strike all the firstborn in Egypt. Now the blood shall be a sign on your houses. When I see the blood, I will pass over you; and the plague shall not destroy you when I strike Egypt.*9

The blood on the doorpost said, "The wrath of God already visited this house. Death was here. Pass over this house." This blood on the doorpost of the world means that pardon is free to any and all who choose to accept it. This Blood of The Lamb marks our offenders. Seeing only the precious blood of our Savior, we stop looking for any lower justice. We pass over that blood-marked person by imitating our Father.

How Papa Does It

How does our Father forgive? He sees the blood of Christ, the Lamb, and passes over those touched by this blood. He looks at the crucified Christ, and declares the debt paid. How then shall we forgive? We shall look to the blood of Christ, pass over the offence and the offender, and declare the penalty paid. The blood

Jesus shed for the sins we committed against others was also shed for the sins others committed against us. As the Father looks upon Christ and is satisfied, so we too look upon Christ and are satisfied. Did He die to satisfy us? No. He died to clear us of our trespasses, but He also died to clear those who trespass against us. He satisfied God's justice. Surely, if it is satisfactory to God, it must be satisfactory to us. The sin committed against me was paid for by the death of Jesus Christ. My spirit, *joined to the Holy Spirit*,10 forgives by looking at the cross of Christ.

This works because God has given you faith in the blood of Christ. This works because Christ **is** your faith. This faith is already in your heart; put there by the grace of God. This works because you are a new creation in Christ Jesus, created to forgive. This is how your God does it, and this is the way He made for you to do it. This works because the God who is forgiving through you is doing it this way.

On Calvary's dark day, Jesus presented His sacrifice to His Father asking Him to forgive us. The Word of God presents us with the blood shed for our offenders, and asks us to forgive them. We look upon it, bow to His love, and forgive those for whom He spilt His blood. Like Jesus, we bring this blood to our Father asking Him to have mercy on our foes for whom Christ died. Do we have something better to offer? Surely, we know we are not better than God that we should forgive without the death and suffering of Christ. This is how Papa does it, honoring the sacrifice of His Son, He looks to the cross as He forgives our sins. So then, imitating this, we forgive with His forgiveness. We acknowledge the offence punished on Calvary, forgiving all because they **are** forgiven. It is enough. It is finished.

Christ our Passover is sacrificed for us.

Therefore let us keep the feast.

Alleluia, Alleluia.11

Earlier I told you that God, as a master builder, is building a house for us. From foundation to weather vane, the only material He used is love. We have entered this House of Forgiveness;12 now let's look around...

1Matthew 6:12; 2John 8:36; 3Matthew 16:19; 4Ephesians 4:32; 5Ephesians 5:1; 6Matthew 18:3; 7Exodus 5:1; 8Psalm 105:36; 9Exodus 12:12; 101Corinthians 6:17; 11Book of Common Prayer; 12Chapter one/Good News

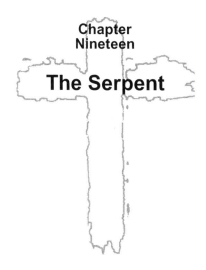

Chapter
Nineteen

The Serpent

Road-weary and battle-worn, the children of Israel were deeply discouraged. They complained about the steady diet of manna and murmured against God and Moses. The momentum of their grumble carried them across the line when they accused God of plotting to desert them. Silent judgment slipped into the camp in the form of little fiery venomous snakes. *And they bit the people; and many people of Israel died.*

A most sincere apology quickly ensued, along with an urgent request for help. *"We have sinned, for we have spoken against the Lord, and against you. Pray unto the Lord, that he take away the serpents from us."*

And the Lord said to Moses, "Make a fiery serpent, and put it on a pole. Here is what will happen: every one bitten, who looks at it, shall live." So Moses made a serpent of brass, put it upon a pole, and it happened that if a serpent bit anyone, when they looked to the serpent of brass, they lived. And the children of Israel moved on…[1]

This story works as a parable for the act of forgiveness. A wound from a conflict is like snakebite killing our joy, our peace, our relationships, and sometimes our bodies. We cry out for God to remove those who offend us, but instead He shows us some-thing that neutralizes the venom of rancor. Jesus compared Him-self on the cross to the serpent up on the pole, giving life to all who see Him. He said, *"As Moses lifted up the brass snake in the desert, so must the Son of man be lifted up."*[2]

Allegory

Christ is presenting an allegory for us. He claims to be like the snake because on the cross He became the curse. *Christ has redeemed us from the curse of the law, being made a curse for us: for it is written, "Cursed is every one that hangs on a tree."*[3] A serpent is a biblical symbol for sin, evil and the curse: *The Lord God said to the serpent, "Because you have done this, cursed are you..."*[4]

But let's be clear: Jesus has no similarity to the tempter who worked through a snake in the Garden of Eden. Satan was a creature taking the world away into sin; Christ is the creator tak-ing away the sin of the world. Lifted on the Roman torture rack, He is a vision of God's wrath on the slithering snake that is our iniquity. *For God made him who knew no sin, to be sin for us.*[5]

When Christ is mounted on the cross, He is all sin: our sin and the sin of our tormentors –– sins we commit and those com-mitted against us. He is any sin committed at any time by anyone. More than that, He is us. He is the fallen beast that humanity has become. On that eternal hill, He lives it all. From the first breath of Adam to the death rattle of the last sinner on earth, He suffers it.

Matthew's eyewitness account: *"Now from the sixth hour there was darkness over all the land unto the ninth hour."*[6] The darkness of the ages is brought to the one point in time that is the whole point of time. *In the right time Christ died for the ungodly.*[7] The death that gathers on Golgotha, is so thick it darkens the skies over Jerusalem as it lands on the Son of God. The Prophet Isaiah said, *"All we like sheep have gone astray; we have turned every one to his own way; and the Lord has laid on him the iniq-uity of us all."*[8] He suffers our pain, sin and death in ways impos-sible for us to comprehend. It is our cry that tears His soul when He screams, *"Why have you forsaken me?"*[9]

Through the prophet-psalmist, the Spirit gives us an inner glimpse of the tormented Savior lamenting prayerfully, *"But I am a worm, and no man."*[10] This worm, like the brass snake lifted up in the desert of history, is the God of those who lose their humanity – both victim and perpetrator. This Man hangs writhing beneath the black skies of God's wrath for those who strike us with poison. If we would be healed of their sting, we must look not at them, but at the cross-fixed Christ on whom justice is exacted. Fully punished, *the brass serpent*, nailed to the cross of Calvary quenches the venomous fire that burns our souls.

Just Look

Though it took very little faith to glance at the pole-mounted snake above the tents in the middle of camp, the passage infers that some people passed on the cure. The *mustard seed* amount of trust that was enough to save the afflicted is enough to save us from the sting of resentment. We look to the cruel tree that Jesus planted on the hill and we are healed by the faith God planted in our hearts.

After comparing Himself to the brass serpent, Jesus went on to say, *"That whoever believes in him should not perish, but have eternal life."*[11] At first reading, it does not appear He is talking about enabling us to forgive, but look closer. The life He offers includes forgiveness: it brings our mercy to life. The faith by which we are redeemed, and by which we have eternal life, is the same faith by which we forgive. This forgiveness is an expression of that *eternal life* who is in us. He who is our life is our forgiveness. Christ forgives us that we might forgive, so that whoever believes in him does not perish with the bite of unforgiveness, but has an on-going life of love. Our salvation is far from an isolated religious occurrence in our past. It is Christ living, loving, and forgiving in us now.

Ask

And the people said to Moses, "Pray unto the LORD, that He take away the serpents from us." Like so much of Christianity, it is about calling on God. We must ask God to give us the vision of Jesus on the Cross. What takes away the stinging toxin of malice is the sight of faith. *Therefore I say unto you, what things so ever you desire, when you pray, believe that you receive them, and you shall have them.*[12] If you ask for the vision it shall be given to you. It is that simple. James contends that our *warring and fighting* come because we do not petition God for the things He wants for us, "*You have not because you ask not.*"13 Even so, it is in you now. You have the vision. You see it in your mind's eye even now.

John the Baptist, pointing to Jesus, referred to another animal symbol for the sacrificed Christ. *"Look at the Lamb of God,"* he said, *"Who takes away the sin of the World."*14 As we look at Jesus on the cross, the sin of our world is taken away. The Lamb removes the sin of others from our view.

Some say, "Love is blind." That is not true. It is just that *Love covers all sins.*15 Those who hurt us are hidden behind the sweet vision of the Lamb, the Christ Crucified, who calls Himself the healing *"Serpent."* He *takes away the sin of the world*…it is gone. We saw Christ drag it away, and slay it on the high mount. *It is finished.* It's not there. We walk on because the obstacle is removed – gone – nothing there to remember or forget. All that remains is forgiveness.

*"And the children of Israel moved on…"*16 Looking to Him who is our Cure, we too fold the tents of our complaint, leave our hate-infested, soul-toxic encampment, and move on.

And now let's talk about moving beyond the need for retaliation…

[1]Numbers 21:5-10; [2]John 3:14; [3]Galatians 3:13; [4]Genesis 3:14; [5]2 Corinthians 5:21; [6]Matthew 27:45; [7]Romans 5:6; [8]Isaiah 53:6; [9]Mark 15:34; [10]Psalm 22:6; [11]John 3:16; [12]Mark 11:24; [13]James 4:2; [14]John 1:29; [15]Proverbs 10:12 ; [16]Numbers 21:10

Jeff Quill

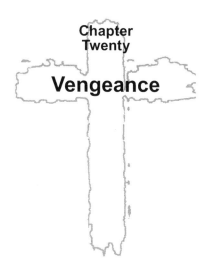

Chapter
Twenty

Vengeance

Vengeance Is Mine. Hebrews 10:30

Once upon a time, in a land not so far away, a woman merrily whistled a tune as she hung clothes outside on the line to dry. After she went into the house, a gust of wind blew all the clothes off the line and into the mud. When she came out to take down the dry clothes, she screamed at the sight of hours of hard work driven into the muck. Picking up the clothes, she returned to the creek and rewashed everything. She pounded the cloth harder and harder as she seethed over her misfortune; hitting one piece so hard it tore. That beat the limit. She looked up toward the house at the trees blowing in the wind. Growling like a mad dog, she hiked her skirt, ran up the hill to the yard, and with everything her mouth could produce, she spit directly into the wind...several times.

One problem with our vengeance is that ultimately it hurts us. Because our Father hates to see us hurt like that, He assigns love to us who are best at revenge, and assigns revenge to Him who is best at love, that is, Himself. He claims exclusive rights to payback.

We know Him who said, "Vengeance is Mine, I will repay."[1]

We were all slated for the wrath of Him who loves us and yet holds all rights to recompense. Once again God stood in the dilemma only He could resolve. It is His prerogative to do with vengeance as He chooses; He chose to strike Himself instead of us.

Many times the Bible calls God our *"Shield."* Of all the dangers from which He shields us, none is greater than His own holy justice. He absorbs the blow of recompense on His cross. Vengeance – the damages exacted for our crimes – could not be satisfied in any way but by the blood of the cross, so He handled it Himself. Only God can satisfactorily answer to God. Just as *He swore by Himself because He could find no greater,*2 so He Himself answered the call for justice because He could find none greater. Only the Lamb is found worthy to open the seals of God's judgment because only the Lamb is equal to it. And they sang a new song, *"You are worthy to take the book, and to open the seals: for You were slain, and redeemed us to God by your blood, out of every family, and language, and race and nation."*3

Vengeance due us comes down on the Son of God who keeps it all to Himself and on Himself. But just as surely, He also takes upon His own person the revenge due to our enemies.

Is It Enough?

You can now let go of vengeance, because the punishment for crimes against you is administered to God the Son. The word of God presents His suffering and death to your offended heart. Christ extends nail-pocked hands asking, "Is this enough?" Well, is it? You know it is. As He said to Thomas, *"Put your finger in My wounds and your hand in My side, and be no more unbelieving, but believing,"*4 He is saying to you, "Come look at My hands and My side, and be no more unforgiving, but forgiving." Read the sentence of your offender, scrawled by a cat o' nine tails across your precious Savior's back; it will melt you into forgiveness. "Enough! Enough! It is enough." The new heart He created in you can do nothing else, and the old nature can do nothing at all.

The question is: How highly do you value the blood of Jesus Christ? If this is not enough for my foe, it is not enough for me. The sacrifice insufficient for one is not sufficient for any. The body not broken for everyone is broken for no one. If you clearly see what pains He suffered for the harm inflicted on you, you can only forgive.

We have faith in this blood. A faith *not of ourselves, it is the gift of God.*5 That is why we forgive when we view the cross. We believe in Him. We forgive by our faith in the blood of Jesus, shed for the sin of those who do us wrong. *And the Spirit bears witness with our spirit,*6 as He forgives through us. We cannot fail in this, for He is our success.

Honesty.

Still, the desire for retribution served up bloody, burns in the human gut. The more we resist the urge for vengeance the stronger it becomes. Resistance can strengthen a bad thing. Some say we are to beat the resentment down, but with what shall we pound it? In the Psalms, shocking rage pours out before God. *"Destroy all them that afflict my soul,"*7 is one of the milder requests. David prayed against his enemies, calling for God's wrath, *"Set a wicked man over him: and let Satan stand at his right hand when he shall be judged. Let him be condemned: and let his prayer become sin."*8

Some of his calls are worse than this. Standing before his God, he did not pretend to be something he was not. Knowing his anger was not hidden from his Lord, he confessed it, and actually tried to enlist the Most High in his cause. I fancy that *the times of this ignorance God winked at,*9 and with tongue in cheek, said, "Oh, sure, David; I'll get right on that."

In a Bible discussion I heard a young man say, "The Lord tells us to pray for our enemies," then he added with a mischievous grin, "But He doesn't say what to pray." The inference was that we could pray down trouble on our foes. When a couple of the Lord's disciples wanted to *"call down fire,"* on some townsfolk, He turned and rebuked them saying, *"You don't know what manner of Spirit you are of."*10 Praying for misfortune is flirting with a dark spirituality. Though He wants to hear how we feel about things, God shows His clear expectation, saying, *"Bless them which persecute you: bless, and curse not."*11

Yet God delighted in the shepherd king who also prayed, *"Behold, You desire truth in the inward parts."*12 Phony, sanctimonious recitations that cloak our anger do not stand with our God.

107

We can be real with Him who invented real, but because we are ashamed of our broiling hostility, we try to cover it up.

Cover up

He that covers his sins shall not advance, but whoever confesses and forsakes them shall have mercy.[13] Burying anger out of sight gets us nowhere. It is like the man who tried to rid his house of rats by using poison. It killed the rats, but he could not find all the carcasses, and some began to stink. He couldn't invite any one to dinner until he found every last rodent. Anger stuffed away puts a stench in the soul. It can cause an ugly, snappy attitude. Solomon warns: *"Anger settles deep into the bosom of fools."*[14] It is best to lay it out before Him, knowing that *all things are naked and opened to the eyes of Him with whom we have to do.*[15] We can confess the need for revenge – with a passion for obliteration – for God knows what anger burns within us. Anger seeks a punished object. We have a punished object. The God of vengeance asks us to stand before the suffering Christ who died for the object of our anger, and let our resentment fall into the mud made by holy blood. Those who *afflict our souls* disappear into the crucified person of the Second Person. Our seething wrath sinks beneath the cleansing stream drawn from the veins of love. Once we admit the desire, we look upon the cross where our demand for justice is obliterated in the battered body of Christ Himself. Look, be satisfied, and drop the grudge. God poured out His wrath on Christ to avenge the wrongs done to us by others, and also to punish our own hatred. Not only do we get-even in the cross, we get right with God.

Mad At God

Many of us are angry with God for the way things worked out for us. I know a couple that lost a precious child after a long and painful illness. It was years before they could speak a civil word to God. A friend of my youth used to stand outside and shake his fist at heaven for the dysfunction of his family. We don't like to admit it, even to ourselves, but sometimes we feel God did us wrong. He didn't. Our God can do no evil. If you think He should be punished for the state of this world, you are mistaken. But if it helps you, punished He was – for everything. With aching heart, He waits for you to come to Him that He may comfort you.

The fire of a vindictive spirit may burn our souls beyond feeling, but it will not quench our thirst for revenge – only the cross will do that. The friends and families of murder victims sometimes witness the perpetrator's execution. They commonly report that, while it could not bring back their loved one, it **did** bring back their pain afresh. They say it did nothing to soothe the hurt, close the wound or satisfy their need for justice. Only the vision of Christ crucified does that. Christ shall heal the wounds, satisfy justice and bring all back to life;16 The one of whom it is prophesied, *"He shall execute judgment and justice in the earth,"* is the same one who says, *"I am the resurrection and the life."*17 He shall one day raise all of us from the dead.

Christ suffered all punishment and absorbed all due retribution. He shall also restore all to life, and make more than full restitution for our losses. The happily penitent Zacchaeus promised Jesus, *"If I have taken any thing from any man by false accusation , I restore him fourfold."* That is impressive.18 Yet Christ promises, *"an hundredfold now in this time, houses, and brethren, and sisters, and mothers, and children, and lands, after persecutions; and in the world to come eternal life."*19 This promise can only be understood if you *Set your affection on things above...where Christ sits... not on things on the earth,*20 *for where your treasure is , there will your heart be also.*21 Christ is the restoration *"after persecutions"* both here and hereafter.

Consider Paul the Apostle. This man was stalked by assassins and slanderers. He was laughed off the stage by the intellegencia of Athens. He was stoned and left for dead at Lystra; beaten imprisoned and secured in stocks in Philippi, and defamed throughout the Mediterranean area. Besides all that, he probably suffered from an acutely painful eye malady. Yet he tells us, *"I reckon that the sufferings of this present time are not worthy to be compared with the glory which shall be revealed in us."*22 Christ will infinitely more than make up for what we suffer. *And God shall wipe away all tears from their eyes; and there shall be no more death, neither sorrow, nor crying, neither shall there be any more pain: for the former things are passed away.*23 Our vengeance could never bring all this about. His vengeance goes beyond punishment to unthinkable blessing. All we go through He also endures, and all we lose He restores to a degree that leaves our greatest losses unworthy of mention. Knowing this, Paul said, *"I count all things but loss for the supremacy of the knowledge of Christ Jesus my Lord: for whom I have suffered the loss of all things, and do count them as so much manure, in order that I may win Christ."*[24]

And now let us see how this Lamb who's love breaks the cycle of vengeance also breaks through our darkness and heals our blindness...

[1]Hebrews 10:30; [2]Hebrews 6:13; [3]Revelation 5:9; [4]John 20:27; [5]Ephesians2:10; [6]Romans 8:16; [7]Psalms 143:12; [8]Psalm 109:6-7; [9]Acts 17:30; [10]Luke9:54,55; [11]Romans 12:14; [12]Psalms 51:6; [13]Proverbs28:13; [14]Ecclesiastes7:9; [15]Hebrews4:13; [16]John 5:25; [17]John 11:25; [18]Luke 19:8; [19]Mark10:30; [20]Colossians 3:1; [21]Luke2:34; [22]Romans 8:18; [23]Revelation 21:4; [24]Philippians 3:8

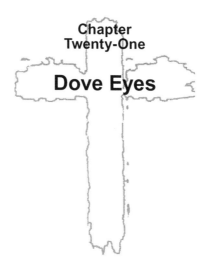

Chapter
Twenty-One

Dove Eyes

For we walk by faith, not by sight. 2Corinthians 5:7

Jesus told the religious teachers of the time, *"Abraham, rejoiced to see my day: and he saw it and was glad."*

They objected, *"You are not yet fifty years old, and have you seen Abraham?"*

Jesus answered, *"Very truly, I tell you, before Abraham was, I Am."*[1]

Abraham was dead and gone many centuries before the Nazarene stood in Jerusalem, and we were out of town at the time; yet, like Abraham, we rejoice to see His day right here, right now. The *"I Am,"* plants the same faith in our hearts as He planted in the heart of the old patriarch.

The proverb "seeing is believing," did not work out for the eyewitnesses who rejected Jesus. Hundreds of miles away few, if any, Galatians met the Nazarene; yet Paul tells them, *"Before your eyes Jesus Christ has been clearly portrayed, crucified among you."*[2] Their vision came not from a first hand, real time view of Golgotha, but from hearing the gospel of light.

Spiritual Sight

How do we know Him or see Him? Simon the fisherman declared before all the disciples that he knew Jesus was *the Christ, the Son of the living God.*

Jesus answered him, *"Blessed are you, Simon Bar Jonah: because flesh and blood has not revealed this unto you, but my Father who is in heaven."*[3]

This is not something Simon figured out, and neither did any of us. Our fleshly minds, hostile to God, cannot think a way into this blessedness of Bar Jonah. The false self will always find a way to avoid the Truth. God alone unveils the Christ for us.

This is the Lord's doing; it is marvelous in our eyes.[4]

The revelation of the Son of God – the "Aha!," the "Yes I see it!" – is a gift from our loving Father working in us by the Holy Spirit. The epiphany of Simon Peter is the loving touch of God's grace. If we want this, our Lord encourages us, *"Ask, and it shall be given unto you."*[5] Getting what we truly need is most often a simple matter of asking.

He who gives us a vision of Christ crucified also gives us a new vision of each other. As God sees us through the blood of Christ, so too, we may see and forbear one another. When we look through the eyes of the Spirit, we see through the blood of Jesus Christ. Why did God make dove eyes red? He surely knew the dove would represent the Holy Spirit of peace and mercy.

Elaina

Let me tell you a story about a friend of mine. We'll call her "Elaina." Her husband, in an act of complete selfishness, left her and the children. As a single parent in a new town, she struggled to support her kids and also her mother. First she found a church home where the family could be grounded in God's word, then, being a well-educated medical professional, she found work at a local hospital.

A year later Elaina struggled with a new hurt – the shabby treatment she received at her new church. Her pastor and his wife spoke to her with saccharine-sweet looks of pity and condescension, patronizing her as a charity case. Worst of all, as she was of minority ethnicity, was the tenor of obnoxious, racially demeaning undertones. Anyone's pride would burn with such treatment. Pastors are in a singular position to do great hurt to many open and trusting hearts.

In dread, she avoided them because she could barely conceal her disappointment and aggravation. A friend told her, "When you meet them, just see the cross in front of them. Look at them as though you were looking through a transparent cross."

During a retreat, as Elaina walked in meditation on the beach, the pastoral couple came walking from the opposite direction. "Nowhere to run. Lord, please help me see them through your cross," She prayed. When they finally stood before her on the sand, she pictured the clear cross in front of them and was surprised by the affection welling up for them. They were heartened and edified just by talking with her. Ecstatic joy overtook her as she walked on praising the Lamb of God who takes away the sin of the shepherds.

Shackles and Glue

The soreness of emotional, psychological, and spiritual wounds can bind us to our enemies like a ball and chain. Our Lord does not want us dragging dead weight. He carried the weight of the world on His shoulders so that it would not crush us or hold us back from His joy. The chain snaps as we look to the crucified Christ instead of looking to the seeming caustic person troubling us.

The story is told of how Br're Fox caught Br're Rabbit by making a figure of tar and putting it on the side of the road. Passing by, Br're Rabbit saw the decoy and fell to bickering with it. True to his nature, in a fit of vengeful rage, he assaulted the mute, sticky effigy. Of course, he got stuck in the tar and was captured by Br're Fox. Struggles with tar dummies on our road only get us stuck. We become easy prey for misery. Brooding over an injury cements us to that injury, while contemplation of the Christ of Calvary fills our attention, and pulls us away from the tacky snags on our journey. Eyes to the Christ who was bound for all keeps us unbound and at peace. *If the Son therefore shall liberate you,* (from the grippy stickums of rehashed offences) *you shall in fact be free.*6

The torment reserved for our foes appears upon Jesus like thorns on a crown. We are not called to wear the thorns of malice

115

on our heads, but a *helmet of salvation*.7 The wounds on His head weep with the bad blood of our offenders; His skull burns under our smoldering grudge; He is afflicted that we might know His peace. We look to His agony, and let go of ours.

Marathoners

Look unto me and be liberated, all the ends of the earth.8 The Bible exhorts us to look unto Jesus, keeping our eyes on Him during the long distance run through this life. *Let us lay aside every weight, and the sin which so easily engulfs us, and let us run with patience the race that is set before us, turning our eyes and fixing them on Jesus the author and finisher of our faith*.9

Our sin throws us off the pace, but also the sin committed against us breaks our stride. The weight of animosity holds us back. Looking to Him who gave us our faith, we can move ahead. That faith, by which we see and forgive, is authored and finished by Jesus Christ on Calvary. It all comes from *fixing our eyes on Jesus*. Seeing Him on the hilltop shouting to us, *"It is finished,"* we believe Him. We survey the wondrous cross 10 that punished the wrongs we suffered. Posting our accusation on that timber, we leave it, and go on with the race. It is a race into the center of God's heart.

On your mark – get set – forgive. Last one there is nothing but love.

[1]John 8:56-58; [2]Galatians 3:1; [3]Matthew16:16-17; [4]Psalm118:23; [5]Matthew7:7; [6]John8:36; [7]Ephesians6:17; [8]Isaiah 45:22; [9]Hebrews 12:1-2 [10]When I Survey The Wondrous Cross-C.Wesley

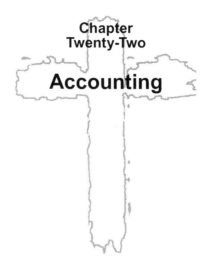

Chapter
Twenty-Two

Accounting

A hundred years or so after Christ, someone wrote a fictional work about the apostle Thomas. In the story, the Lord directs Thomas to travel to a certain country. Thomas refuses. The Lord then, disguised as a slave trader, sells Thomas to a king from the nation He wanted him to serve. A funny yarn, but it reminds me of Paul's point: *"What? Don't you know that… you are not your own? For you are bought with a price."*[1]

Everyone is the property of God. He paid an incomprehensible price for us, *You were not redeemed with perishables: silver and gold…but with the precious blood of Christ.*[2] By value, a drop of this blood out weighs the world. It is by this leverage precisely that He owns all and has the right to forgive all. The imperishable blood that clears all debts and all charges against us also clears all debts and all charges against those who hurt us. The blood purchased all we have, and all we are. It also purchased everything our debtors have and everything our debtors are.

The debt is not owed to us anymore; it is owed to Christ. That which is most harmful to us – unforgiveness toward our debtors – is removed in the realization that nothing is owed to us anymore.

Collectors

As a young man I once worked for a delightfully eccentric inventor. His clothes were always a bit shabby and his hair resembled the locks of Albert Einstein. He came up with a kids' toy that he believed could finance all his other "more serious" projects. I never saw a man work harder, but the market was just not there. The man I felt sorry for, though, was the old navy veteran who rented out his house to this entrepreneur. Putting on his best landlord face, he came to the house one evening looking strong, resolute, and ready to collect months of back rent. The genius, with mind-numbing zeal, showed him the toy, the bright packaging, the big leads, and the bigger ideas for other inventions. Exhorting like a tent evangelist, he urged his creditor to believe in the vision. After an hour of the inventor's verbal bombardment, the poor landowner – head bowed and shoulders slumped – looked as though he were about to cry.

"I came over here determined to get my money or get you out of here, and now all I can think of is this confounded child's toy." He staggered out of the house into the bleak winter night.

After many months of no pay, I too moved on, but I had a new appreciation of those who must collect debts. It is very often a frustrating and thankless task. Christ frees us from the curse of debt collection. We need not bother with that nuisance. Understanding that the debt is already paid, will help us to let it go.

Debt

Though I use the landlord and the inventor as an illustration, we are not referring here to financial debt. That is a discussion for another day. The debt we mean is expressed in sayings like, "He paid his debt to society," or "I owe you an apology," or the threats – "Someday he will get what's coming to him," or "Someday you will pay for this." It is what we understand as a moral or spiritual debt.

Let us revisit Jesus' parable of the unforgiving servant. As you recall, a king forgave his servant a million dollars. But the same man found a fellow servant who owed him a few dollars, took him by the throat, and said, "Pay up." Unable to collect, he threw him into prison. Other servants told their lord what they witnessed.

The king said, *"You rotten servant, I forgave you; you should also forgive."* He delivered the man to the tormentors, till he should, *"pay up."*[3]

All in the story are slaves: the king owned them. The Greek word here for "servant" is better rendered "slave" – a person owned by another. There we stand: we are all owned. The debtor, the creditor, the "fellow servants," and the debt, all belong to God. He may do with them as He wishes. Anything we might use to pay Him already belongs to Him. Having nothing to offer Him, accepting His forgiveness is our only viable option.

The *rotten* slave was freely forgiven. He did nothing to earn this mercy. Before he angered the king, he was fully absolved. Even after he ran afoul of his master, the noble benefactor did not go back on his word. What he forgave the slave was still forgiven. The debt the slave was ordered to pay is the debt he chose to retain, that is, the few dollars he tried to choke out of his fellow slave. Forgiveness from God is never retracted.

Irrevocable Reprieve

One who comes to me I will by no means throw out. (I will never push away)[4] "No means" means "no means," and "never" is "never." Period. There is no such thing as "a most singular exception given the unique conditions of an extremely rare occasion." We are saved from the wrath of God; under no circumstance will that punishment revisit us. As Paul assures us, *"God never changes His mind, and takes back the gifts He gives us."*[5]

Though God requires an accounting of what He gives us, His pardon is never revoked. The amount the slave was sentenced to pay was what he believed was not forgiven. We may try to choose what is or is not forgiven; any debt we retain will stick to us as though it were ours. By not forgiving, we lay claim to the other person's sin. Jesus paid off the debts of our debtors. Ask yourself, "Do I want to pay for the wrong which this or that person did?" The answer, of course, is "No." That debt, existing only in our vindictive misery, will torment us until we find a way to release it, and of course we release it by acknowledging that Jesus already paid for it. Our tormentors are the physical diseases and social wrecks caused by bitterness and resentment. These tormentors shadow us till we let go of what we call, "our just due."

121

Even so, because God loves us, He sees to it that we do not destroy ourselves. He will use our foolishness to straighten us out. It may hurt the temporal outer beast, but it will not harm the inner eternal being.[6] *For whom the Lord loves he disciplines.*[7]

Relieved of Duty

Thank God for setting you free from your debtors. If ever there was a time to pass the buck, this is it. Rather than your debtor's bill showing up in your mailbox, forward it on to Jesus; let it stop with Him. The debt is His; He will take care of it. You are officially dismissed from the role of moral bill collector.

Christ purchased all that is owed to you. All your accounts receivable (things other people owe you) transfer to Him, and belong to God. He paid the debts of all who have done you wrong. Forgiveness begins simply with your acknowledgement that this is true: all is His. The person who did that terrible thing to you does not owe you anything; He owes it to God. Whatever you have, whatever you are, and whatever is owed to you belongs to a God who is ready to forgive it all. Those who do you evil are His, and forgiveness waits for them. Christian forgiveness is the admission of this fact. All is forgiven, and what's more, it is forgiven from your heart. Your Lord, from your heart, forgives all.

The Impenitent

You may wonder, "What if the culprit does not repent? Is he still forgiven?" So far as you and your Lord are concerned, yes. The guilty must accept it to realize the benefits. If he does not take it (much to the grief of the Holy Spirit) he does not have it. You have it in your heart, though. You are ready to release it to whoever needs it. It will astound you what enormous bills you are willing to burn once your debtor asks forgiveness. God has done something amazing in you. We need not bother over whether or not the pardon-seeking perpetrator is truly penitent. That is a matter between him and his God. God just wants us to be free of care. It is not for us, but for God to judge who is or is not earnest. While *The Lord is close to them that are broken-hearted; and saves those of a contrite spirit,* we need only remit forgiveness to those who ask it.

A distressed parent once lamented to me that his family was in turmoil because one of his daughters refused to forgive

122

the other because she doubted the sincerity of her sister's apology. We are not constables of the heart. But rather, we are those who have received such abundant mercy that there is not room enough to contain it. We must give it away. We give God's forgiveness to those whose debts He has paid, without judging their worthiness of it. If forgiveness is allowed me only if I attain to a certain threshold of remorse, I am in jeopardy. Mercy acquired by the blood-investment of Jesus Christ, requires no contribution or worthiness on my part; only acceptance. *If You, Lord, should keep track of imperfections, O Lord, who shall stand ?*[8] By His perfection we stand forgiven, with all our imperfections.

Before he died, Steven cried out, *"Lord, lay not this sin to their charge"*.[9] To whose account then does He lay their sin? It is put to the same account as our sin: it is accounted to Jesus Christ. The Lamb who is slain for **us** is also slain for **them**. When we count people forgiven, it is because they are in fact forgiven. Whether or not they take advantage of that forgiveness is yet another question.

The Receipt

Your forgiveness is not a groundless cancellation of debt out of the natural-born goodness of your heart. The payer of record is Jesus Christ. Your forgiveness is the recognition of His payment in full of all that is owed to you. You acknowledge payment, and then close and discard the account. Unless you wish to retain someone else's debt, all ledgers are clear. The red ink of their sin is blotted out by indelible blood. Look, be satisfied, and drop the debt from your books.

Facing the slightest irritation or the deepest wound, we say, "Jesus paid dearly for this. It is enough." Let us stay at the cross until our souls bow to the truth.

When Jesus pays your brothers debt, all that remains for you is to give a notice of payment: an acknowledgement that the bill is paid in full, an acceptance of what was done. An excellent way to do this is to give thanks to God for the settlement. "Thank You, Lord – it is finished." Out of your hands, off your heart, and no longer your concern, the debt is paid. Let go now. The matter is finished and not worth dwelling on, other than to admire the magnificent way Christ balanced the books. Another great hymn:

> Jesus paid it all.
> All to Him I owe.
> Sin had left a crimson stain.
> He washed it white as snow.[10]

1Corinthians 6:19-20; 2Peter 1:18-19; 3Matthew 18:23-35;4John 6:37; 5Romans11:29; 61Corinthians 3:15, 1Corinthians5:5; 7Hebrews12:6; 8Psalm130:3; 9Acts7:60; 10Jesus Paid It All–E.Hall

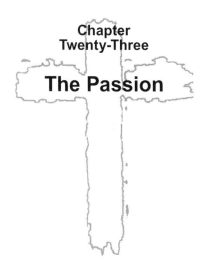

Chapter
Twenty-Three

The Passion

I find it helpful when forgiving, to read through the Gospel accounts of the passion of Christ, because as the psalmist observes, *"The opening of Your Word becomes light and understanding to the opening mind. Your word is a lamp for a light on my foot path."*[1]

As I follow Jesus up the path to Calvary, He lights my way, shows me His love, and walks me through His forgiveness. I approach the Mount of Olives remembering that just as Christ gave all to forgive my trespasses, He also suffered for those who trespass against me. He was punished for what my transgressor did to me, He gave His eye for an eye, and His tooth for a tooth.[2] Though I am guilty of too much to mention, I am looking to the cross for those who have done me wrong, that I may forgive them. I hope those whom I have wronged will do the same.

Here are stories of friends who have followed Jesus up the hill of Calvary all the way to forgiveness.

Katy

Health problems plagued Katy from birth. Now on crutches, the short ten-year-old girl struggled down the steps of the school bus trying not to fall or drop her book bag. Howls of laughter pursued her from inside the vehicle. "Look at the bug. Hey buggy bug," shrieked the tormenting boys over and over. Standing alone on the side of the rode in the cloud of dust and exhaust, she sobbed uncontrollably.

What shall be done to those boys to make up for this?

They spat upon Him, took a reed, and struck Him on the head. After they mocked Him; they ... led Him away... They crucified Him... And passers-by reviled Him, wagging their heads, "If You are the Son of God, come down from the cross." Likewise chief priests, scribes and elders, mocked Him, "He saved others; He cannot save Himself. If He is the King of Israel, let Him comedown from the cross now, and we will believe Him... let God deliver Him now, if He will have Him." The thieves crucified with Him, also ridiculed Him.[3]

Is it enough? It is too much. To Katy's heart it was more than enough.

Mickey

The nuns at St Joseph's Orphanage were wonderful women of God. But every institution has its bad eggs. Sister Ann Sebastian should probably never have been accepted into the convent, let alone allowed to care for children. She made the boys bathe in near scalding water, while she watched.

Once, a little, plastic foot broke off a chair in the playroom. No way any of the thirty boys could know when or how it happened. Sister wanted a confession. She ordered the boys to put dried hot peppers in their mouths until some one admitted to it. Finally, good ol' Mickey Zhelber took the blame, sparing the rest of us further torture.

How shall this woman atone for this?

And they stripped Him, and put a scarlet robe on Him. And when they had fashioned a crown of thorns, they put it upon His head, and a reed in His right hand: and they bowed the knee before Him, and mocked Him.[4]

Will that do? It is far beyond what should do. I drop it as though it were burning my hands. I have let it go.

Peter

All His life, Peter looked forward to being a minister. He was in his dream job – teaching at a bible school on the golden prairies of Canada. He was zealous for the doctrines of his church, so it was painful when he uncovered a profound contradiction in their teaching. He discussed it with other teachers at the school and with ministers of other denominations. The esoteric bit of dogma proved to be out of line with Biblical Christian teaching in every other denomination. Peter could no longer honestly teach that line of thought.

But it is a big Bible with plenty of other things to talk about without touching the point of contention. The dean of the school would have none of that. Peter must teach the doctrine or resign. He was crushed as he handed over his ministerial credentials, thanked the dean for the opportunity, and left the campus.

How shall the dean make this right?

*Then the high priest tore his robe, " Do we need any further witnesses? You have heard the blasphemy: what do you think?" And they all condemned Him to be guilty of death. Some began to spit on Him. They covered His face, and punched Him, saying, "Prophesy: Who hit You?" And the servants of the high priest struck Him with the palms of their hands.*5

The spittle and blood reserved for the clergy drip from the face of God. Peter, with his heart broken before his broken Lord, put the actions of the dean out of his mind forever.

Emma

Emma was a dancer who danced before the Lord. She injured her back so severely that she resorted to crawling when she was home. During those hard days her husband could not find it in himself to care for her. Instead, he began an extramarital affair, informing Emma, "God told me to divorce you."

She had always completely trusted her husband in spiritual things, now she was devastated. She lost her husband, and it appeared her God also forsook her. Lying on the floor in agony and pain, she thought she was actually in hell.

How can this man pay for what he did?

While Jesus was speaking, Judas, one of the twelve came with a great multitude carrying swords and staves. He had given them a sign, saying, "Whoever I kiss, that is he; take him, and lead him away safely."

As soon as he arrived, he went straight to Jesus, and said, "Master, master," and kissed him.

Jesus said, "Judas, do you betray the Son of Man with a kiss?"[6]

And around three pm Jesus cried with a loud voice, saying, "My God, my God, why have You forsaken me?"[7]

At the sight of her forsaken Savior, who knew her agony better than she knew it herself, Emma released her cruel ex-husband from blame. She was now *married to another, even to him who is raised from the dead.*[8] She purchased a simple gold band to wear on her finger.

Mark

The Wheshieme family owned a delicatessen on Berlin Square. In 1939 Mr. Wheshieme sent his son Mark to America as evil began gripping Germany. Once there, Mark joined the U.S. Army. He was used as a spy for the allies during WWII because he spoke German fluently, and knew the country. Wounded before he could reach Berlin, he was sent back to America. None of his family survived the holocaust.

How shall the SS monsters pay? Would it be enough if each of them died six million deaths? No. Only one man can pay for this.

And they took Jesus, and led Him away. And He carried His cross to a spot called Golgotha, which is Hebrew for "the place of a skull." There they crucified Him, and two others with Him, one on either side with Jesus in the middle. And Pilate wrote a title, and put it on the cross. It read:

JESUS OF NAZARETH THE KING OF THE JEWS.[9]

Accusation titles were always posted above the heads of crucified criminals. The title above the thorned head of Christ is the name of innocent holiness. It covers the sin of the whole world. *Blotting out the handwriting of ordinances that was against us, and contrary to us, He took it out of the way, nailing it to His cross.*[10]

Later in life, Mark came to believe in Jesus. By faith in his Messiah he forgave his many losses, and was known by all for his irrepressible joy. At his memorial service, everyone wore colorful bow-ties to acknowledge his constantly cheerful love.

With these examples in mind, we turn now to other memories...

[1]Psalm 119:105; [2]Exodus 21:24; [3]Matthew 27:30,35,39-42,44; [4]Matthew 27:28,29; [5]Matthew 26:65-68; [6]Luke 22:47-48; [7]Mark 15:34; [8]Romans 7:4; [9]John 19:17-19; [10]Colossians 2:14

Chapter
Twenty-four

The Reprimand

I entered the store to see the manager. "Is he in?" I asked the young woman behind the counter. Scowling at me she growled for all her customers and fellow employees to hear, "Why do you people automatically assume the manager is a 'he'? **She** is upstairs."

This university student, blazing with zeal for the cause de femme, saw a chance to roast the pig, and the apple was in my mouth along with my foot. I mumbled something about the problem with our language. She went on with her public tirade. "Well, your language is hurting me." Touché. Ouch. I was too surprised and humiliated – too defensive to graciously engage her in a meaningful apology. Making some silly, self-effacing comment I shuffled off to find the manager.

A friend once told me, "Every encounter is an opportunity to forgive or be forgiven." I do not doubt it, given the human condition. This small incident demonstrates what God is doing in us.

Years later, sitting in prayer on a park bench, I remembered the incident. Falling into a grousing verbal retaliation, I told her a thing or two.

"Why, why...Oh Yeah? I... and another thing... Lord."

Conscious that I was in the throne room of God, slapping the ghost of a trivial slight, I asked, "Why am I thinking about this stuff, Lord?" It seemed to me that the Holy Spirit brought this to mind through prayer so He could work His forgiveness in me.

Right off I saw that I needed to be forgiven for my inability to receive correction. "But...but...but she reprimanded me in public. Only a saint could respond with grace to an ambush like that." Sainthood is what the Holy seeks in us, isn't it? Our Father holds a high vision of who we are in Christ. In this instance, I definitely came short of the glory of God. Solomon said, *"Rebuke a wise man and he will love you...but fools despise wisdom and instruction."* He recommends, *"beatings for the back of fools."*[1]

"Father, the back of Jesus was beaten for my stubborn heart. Look there, and forgive me."

I gave it little thought as I went about my life, but the pain of that public lecture was a dead raccoon under the back porch of my mind, rotting away till God drug it out for me. Sometimes, brushing a thing off does nothing more than store it out of sight, out of consciousness, where it works against our peace. A tiny sliver left in the pinkie becomes a serious infection. By and by, buried small potatoes become fields of big, ripe Idaho Russets. Little things take root. Forgive them before they grow. Life is more enjoyable that way.

Yet my zealous bookstore clerk was no cherub, nor her antics harmless. However right her point, her method deserved a public nose tweak. "Why I oughta…"

And they spat in His face and beat Him saying, "Prophesy to us, Christ. Who hit you?[2]

"I see, Lord, You were publicly humiliated for her actions. It is enough, Lord. O my Lord, It is too much. I see her forehead anointed with a drop of Your blood. She owes me nothing."

Smolder

Yet the scent of anger lingered in my soul. "What is this, Lord? I forgive. Why am I still bitter?" I began to see myself *in Christ* as though in a coat of invisible light. It worked, I separated from the irk. Feeling sorry for what she did as though I had done it, I asked God to forgive her. The weight lifted. *"This I say then"* said Paul, *"Walk in the Spirit, and ye shall not fulfill the lust of the flesh."*3 You cannot be in the water and out of it at the same time. Cannot be in the house and outside at the same time. Like putting your elbow in your ear, you just cannot do it. Accepting that you are **in Christ,** separates and detaches you from the bad stuff.

This kind of thing happens regularly. If I start getting ritualistic with it though, I find it doesn't help. When practicing forgiveness, we need to give it time in the presence of our Papa. He walks us through it by His Spirit.

Crucified

My anger is crucified with Jesus. I release to Him the sin He went after when He took up the cross. I let it go. If I feel it again, I let it go again. I don't drop it into some great nameless void. No, I release my anger, my sinful self, and my enemy it into the abyss of His wounded side.

At a retreat I attended, we were invited to write on a piece of paper the names of people who wronged us and a phrase or two describing what they did. We were to show it to no one. Then, after a sermon about how it was a good thing to forgive our enemies, we gathered outside the chapel to burn the folded papers in a big metal tub. We stood around the flame and sang a hymn. One fellow got my attention and with cold rage in his eyes he opened his paper for me to read. I got the distinct feeling he wished he were burning the people listed and not just their names. As to whether or not the ceremony was effective, I cannot say. I heard little comment about it afterward. For myself, sending paper and ink into the night air helped little if at all. It would be better to replace the names with the name that is above every name, and let that be the burnt offering. It would be better to see all other names blotted out by the blood of the Lamb. Let them go, not into a misty nebulous nowhere, but into the blood of Jesus Christ.

To honor His passion, I unclench my fist, lift my open hands, and worship His sacrificed person. I release all. He opens my heart and quells my rage in the shadow of the cross.

Now the acts of the sinful nature are obvious, they are:... hatred ...contention...wrath...fits of rage. (all grown from small potatoes) *Those who belong to Christ have crucified the sinful nature with its passions.*4

I affirm this truth: "This anger is broken with the Christ on the cross: like His body, like the sacramental bread of life; this I believe. Jesus dies for me, and my anger dies in Him. *And the blood of Jesus Christ cleanses us from all unrighteousness.*5 It cleanses us from all unforgiveness, and cleanses us from all bitterness, from all that is not He."

A Prayer

With Christ, we are *raised in newness of life*6 to love and forgive. I pray things like this, "Holy Spirit, come live here in the place my anger once occupied; Let Your love fill the shack once owned by hatred. Come be light in my dark house; I am a home purchased for You by the blood of the Son of God, who loved me and gave Himself for me."7

Those who dominate and humiliate us are crowned with thorns on the precious head of the King of Kings. It is enough. Misfortune befalling a foe is not the punishment we seek for him. God warns us not to revel in the hardships of adversaries. *Rejoice not when your enemy falls, and let not your heart be glad when he stumbles.*8 Such gloating shows a lack of class, and God's family is classy.

We seek justice in the cross for any abuse suffered. There our violator's trespass is brutally punished; there justice is perfectly executed; there we are avenged. We are freed to love.

But what about those who may not want our love?...

1Proverbs 9:8; 1:7; 19:29; 7; 2Matthew 26:68d; 3Galatians 5:16; 4Galatians 5:19,20,24; 51John 1:9; 6Romans 6:4; 7Galatians 2:20; 8Proverbs 24:17

Chapter Twenty-Five
Beware of Dogs

The wolf also shall dwell with the lamb, the leopard shall lie down with the young goat, the calf and the young lion and the fatling together; and a little child shall lead them. The cow and the bear shall graze; their young ones shall lie down together; and the lion shall eat straw like the ox. The nursing child shall play by the cobra's hole, and the weaned child shall put his hand in the viper's den. They shall not hurt nor destroy in all My holy mountain, for the earth shall be full of the knowledge of the Lord as the waters cover the sea.[1]

A time will come when the lion and the calf shall lie down together, but until then the lion will just be reclining at dinner. When God gets His way, harmony reigns on the mountain, but if someone loves war, no peace settles up there.

Forgiveness Does Not Condone Evil

Forgiving does not mean overlooking a person's wolf-like ways, that is, their tendency to hurt. If an offender does not repent and ask for pardon, he probably does not want it. A student once asked me, "Why did God forgive David for murder but not Cain?" I answered, "Because Cain did not ask." God's love reached out to both men, only one wanted it. David repented and chose God, while Cain hardened his heart and chose loneliness.[2] I may desire fellowship with a persecutor, but until he repents, we cannot go on as though nothing happened. Forgiving does not mean condoning sin. It does not say of injury, "Oh, that's O.K." and excuse a person's bent for combativeness. So long as he shows no change of heart and behavior toward me, I will bless him with a wide berth in our passing.

Prudence

It is O.K. to be careful around thorny people. Caution is not animosity, nor is prudence condemnation. But since life happens on a battlefield, the same Bible that instructs us, *"Put on...kindness, forbearing one another, and forgiving one another,"* also advises us, *"put on the armor of light, the helmet of salvation, and the breastplate of righteousness."*3 Christ our salvation and our righteousness protects our heads and our hearts. In the Lord's Prayer we pray for God's mercy upon ourselves and upon our enemies. In response, God forgives. Then we ask, *"Lead us not into the trial, but deliver us from evil."*4 In response, He grants us peace.

We all live and work along side abrasive individuals. I have a friend who, when encountering an annoying colleague, acknowledges the invisible Christ filling the space between them. She finds peace in this, if not joy. The Lord becomes her shield. As the Psalmist praises, *"You, O Lord, are a shield to me."*5

If an offender has not repented and asked forgiveness, he has not received it. It is fool-hearty to expose myself to further injury by entering the fellowship of one who wishes to do me harm. Christ endured condemnation in his place, therefore I do not condemn that offender, but I recognize his state of mind as hostile to my health, his belligerence as dangerous to my well-being. I bare no ill to junkyard dogs, but I offer them nothing to chew.

Swine and Canine

He who is *made unto us wisdom* says, *"Give not that which is holy unto the dogs, neither cast your pearls before swine, lest they trample them under their feet, and turn again and rend you."*6 A swine is one who does not value the gift you offer. If you give me a book about poisonous insects to share your love of insects with me, I may appreciate your intention, but not your gift. I would be like a pig with a pearl necklace. Give me mud and slop, I will be happy. Much to the chagrin of my daughter, our dog, Yodi, was just as happy with her prized, fuzzy, bunny rabbit slippers as any other chew toy. Sometimes we just don't get it; we don't cherish what our friends cherish. If our pardon is unwanted, then we wisely keep our distance from the offender for his sake, lest he sin against us again. We risk putting him in real danger of wrongdoing.

Paul asks, *"Who is he that condemns? It is Christ Jesus that died."*[7]

Christ gave his life for my enemy; and I will not be the one to slight those sufferings by calling for damnation. Neither will I make myself unnecessarily vulnerable to hellish behavior. How do you show love to someone who is hostile to you? The same way you pick blackberries: very carefully. *Love your enemy,*[8] but remember that he is your enemy. Don't hate him but don't date him. The Lord's goodness makes us *ready to forgive,*[9] but that does not mean the trespasser is ready to be forgiven.

The Pain In The Neck

Some folks are not happy unless they are in a fight. Mac was an angry little boy. All the kids at the orphanage avoided him because he was constantly bickering and needling. Every day he was on the floor wrestling with someone. I felt sorry for him. Feeling inspired by my patron Saint (Dominic Savio, the boy saint of Turin) I decided to befriend the irritating little guy. After a day of his friendship, boiling with rage, I found myself chasing him down and pounding him.

Though warning us against condemnation, the apostle also cautions us not to associate or dine with the chronically abusive. *I have written to you not to keep company, if any man that is called a brother be a...verbal abuser...with such an one know not to eat.*[10]

Jesus teaches us to regard a man who refuses to reconcile as a person we don't know, or as a disreputable, oppressive tax collector. Seeing the collector afar off, we make ourselves scarce. Some folks just go about collecting trouble. Don't be home when they come calling. *Let him be unto you as a heathen man and a mercenary tax collector.*[11]

Audacity and Imposition

Forgiveness cannot be foisted on anyone. None are compelled to accept pardon. Mercy is gifted to unworthy penitents, not imposed upon the unwilling or indifferent. Jesus said to those who felt no need of forgiveness, *"I came not to call the righteous, but sinners to repentance."*[12]

Some fine and upstanding citizen may find it presumptuous that I have forgiveness to offer. Mercy grates on a bad conscience, and grace agitates repressed guilt. The complacent bristle at the offer of pardon – it presupposes they have sinned. The insult of reconciliation is best left to the Holy Spirit.

Knowing better than to let the ornery prey upon our peace, let's talk about how we may better pray for the peace of the ornery....

1Isaiah 11:6-9; 2Genesis 4:13-16; 3Colossians 3:13, Ephesians 6:14; 4Luke 11:4; 5Psalms 3:3; 61Corinthians 1:30; Matthew 7:6; 7Romans 8:34; 8Matthew 5:44; 9Psalm 86:5; 101Corinthians 5:11; 11Matthew 18:17; 12Luke 5:32.

Chapter Twenty-Six

Prayer

I desire that men pray everywhere, lifting up holy hands, *without punishing anger and contentious doubt.* 1Timothy 2:8

Here is a mental exercise that fires my faith when I feel unworthy to enter God's presence. I picture the wounds of Jesus on my hands as I hold them up to God. Emboldened by the scars on the hands of Jesus, I come into the *Holy Place*.1 This always works for me. It is like Jacob, covering his hand with fur to deceive his blind father, Isaac, into thinking he was not Jacob, but Isaac's elder son Esau.

*So Jacob came close to Isaac his father, and he felt him and said, "The voice is the voice of Jacob, but the hands are the hands of Esau." He did not recognize him, because his hands were hairy like his brother Esau's hands; so he blessed him.*2 The hands of His Son and the voice of this sinner do not trick God the Father, but it tricks me into forgetting my foolishness long enough to enjoy time with my God.

The holy hands we lift are the hands of Jesus. When we come to God in Jesus' name, we come not on the credits of our names, but on the merits of Christ. We stand as Christ saying,

*"Father forgive them."*3 Thus we present His hands. Can we find holier hands than His? Jesus is a great priest4 who lifts His redeeming hands to God in empathy with our weakness.

*Let us come boldly unto the throne of grace, that we may receive kindness, and find grace for help when we need it.*5 Needing His help to forgive, we enter into the sacred throne room, and approach God by the blood of Christ. We look to Him, lift holy hands in surrender, and the Spirit of forgiveness moves in love for us. Prayer is essential to forgiveness, and forgiveness is essentially prayer...

Forgiveness As Intercession

Forgiveness is prayer in which we lose the need for retaliation, and quiet the noisy inner squabbling that spoils our peace. When we see the guilty chastised in the Crucified, we truly love them because we place them in Christ – the highest position in the universe. This is intercession of the purest kind. It is a way to *love your enemies, ... and pray for them which despitefully use you, and persecute you.*6 We leave them to Him. Committing a soul to God's care, by faith, is the greatest blessing we can bestow. They have places in their hearts that only the Spirit can reach.

Praying for someone can activate the faith and love needed to forgive them. Like so many of you, when I was a student, some very nasty high school bullies victimized me. They took full advantage of the naiveté that I brought with me from the orphanage. I am sure you could fill in the story with details of mean behavior that you suffered. For many years, when those days came to mind, I brooded over the abuse and fantasized different outcomes favoring revenge. One morning, during my quiet time, I felt the Spirit pressing me to pray for those young tormentors. As I began to think about what to pray, it became evident that the Lord had been working my soul toward this liberating moment for a long time. How faithful He is! Asking God's best for them and their families released me from old resentments. Because Christ bore their cross, I now bear them no grudge.

The Altar

The old rugged cross was an altar on which God's lamb was sacrificed. In the temple at Jerusalem, anything touching the altar was deemed Holy. *It shall be an altar most holy: whatsoever touches the altar shall be holy.*7 What we put on the altar is holy – that means – separated unto God. The cross is an altar sanctified by the perfect sacrifice. Seeing Christ on that cross, dying for our offenders, is a prayer placing them upon the sacred altar with God. To us they become holy, that is, the wards of God. It is perfect prayer.

Forgiveness as Worship

Forgiveness is an act of worship – an exaltation of the sacrificed Christ who is the name of forgiveness. It is the adoration of the Lamb upon the throne of our hearts. Any mention in the scriptures of *"The Lamb,"* is a reminder that our redemption came at a great cost to God. When we forgive by the Blood of the Lamb, we join *A great multitude, no man could number, of all nations, families, people, and languages, standing before the throne, and before the Lamb, clothed with white robes, and palms in their hands, crying with a loud voice, "Salvation to our God which sits upon the throne, and unto the Lamb."*8

These white robes are free to us but not to God. We are *those who have washed their robes white in the blood of the Lamb.*9 We are those who exult in His extravagant expenditure and exalt His suffering and death. Hallowed be this sacrifice that bought forgiveness for us, brought forgiveness to us, and evokes forgiveness in us.

*And every creature which is in heaven, and on the earth, and under the earth, and such as are in the sea, and all that are in them, I heard saying, "Blessing, and honor, and glory, and power, be unto Him that sits upon the throne, and unto the Lamb for ever and ever."*10

He is exalted because, like a lamb, this Lion11 humbled Himself. He is exalted because, when He found Himself in the shape of a man, *He became obedient unto death*12 – our death, giving us reason to humble ourselves, and become obedient to His life of mercy in our hearts. Because He submitted to the death of the cross to save us, our knees bow at His name, the name of Love, and our tongues confess, to the glory of God the Father, that Jesus Christ is the forgiving Lord within us.12 Nothing honors that name more than our exercise of His mercy toward those who

147

deserve it as little as we. The appearance of His forgiveness in us glorifies His victory on the cross.

Forgiveness and Thanksgiving

A young man studying for the ministry was overwhelmed with gratitude toward his instructors. He asked one teacher, "How can I show appreciation for all you have done for me?"

After a moment she smiled, "If you put into practice the things you have learned, nothing could make me happier."

We best show our gratitude, and please our Master, when we bestow His mercy on our world. The release of His kindness upon our enemies is due thanks for the costly forgiveness God shows us.

Paul teaches that forgiveness leads to, and includes, thankfulness. *Put on…humbleness of mind...forgiving one another…as Christ forgave you…and be thankful, singing with grace in your hearts to the Lord.*13 In this scripture condensation, the apostle shows that joyous thanks grows from Christ's gracious forgiveness. He is the Forgiving Spirit in us all, filling us with a gratitude that makes us live with songs in our hearts. Jesus speaks to us of this loving forgiveness because He seeks our happiness; He wants joy for us. *These things have I spoken unto you, that my joy might remain in you, and that your joy might be full.*14

One thing that helps in the process of forgivenesws is thanksgiving in the face of pain. It is difficult, and may at first seem too hard to practice. But still it helps. From prison, Paul writes to the troubled Philippians, *"Be anxious for nothing, but in **everything** by prayer and supplication, with thanksgiving, let your requests be made known to God; and the peace of God, which surpasses all understanding, will guard your hearts and minds through Christ Jesus."*15 Knowing that God is at work *"in everything"* concerning us, we give thanks even for the wrongs we suffer. This is very hard to do. I know. But He would have us live in carefree peace. Acknowledging the difficulty of giving thanks for our troubles, scripture exhorts, *"By Him therefore let us offer the sacrifice of praise to God continually, that is, the fruit of our lips giving thanks to His name."*16

The sacrifice of thanksgiving takes the power away from our wrongdoers, and returns it to our God. It can free us of emotional entanglement with a problem person. Thanking God in a painful situation may not at first ease that pain, but I have found that almost immediately, something within me shifts from despair to hope, from a shallow weakness to a deep strength, and from apparent defeat to a sure but unseen victory. To the persecuted Thessalonians Paul writes, *"Rejoice always, pray without ceasing, in everything give thanks; for this is the will of God in Christ Jesus for you."*17 This is what God really wants for you: *Love, Joy, and Peace in the Holy Spirit.*18 A thankful heart is a happy heart. Your Papa wants that for you.

The end of it is this: rather than dwelling on the injury, or on those who inflict harm, we turn our eyes toward Jesus, and worship Him. To help us with this, God made a way for our eyes to see the Crucified...

1Hebrews 9:12; 2Genesis 27:22-23; 3Luke 23:34; 4Hebrews 4:15; 5Hebrews 4:16; 6Matthew 5:44; 7Exodus 29:37; 8Revelation 7: 9,10; 9Revelation 7:14; 10Revelation 5:13; 11Hosea 5:14; 12Philippians 2:6-11; 13Colossians 3:11-16; 14John 15:11; 15Philippians 4:6; 16Hebrews 13:15; 171Thessalonians 5:16-18; 18Romans 14:17

**Chapter
Twenty-Seven**

Bread and Wine

By the end of His journey, a large company surrounded Jesus. The crowds pressed in around Him trying to see or touch Him. It was nigh impossible to visit alone with Him. The disciple Philip was one of the few with an inside connection to Jesus. As a Galilean, he knew what it was to be an outsider, so he could sympathize with the outsider Greeks who sought an audience with Christ. They pled with him *"Sir, we would see Jesus."*1.

Our God, who can certainly sympathize with outsiders, has arranged a meeting for us to *"see Jesus."*

Rendezvous With The Master

There are many ways to encounter the crucified Lord. Listening to, or reading the Gospel accounts of the passion of the Christ is one way of bringing the cross into focus for us. Another way is The Fourteen Stations of the Cross. As a boy, I found this a very stirring contemplation of His sufferings. In those days, I thought of Jesus more as my hero-God than my loving Savior. At the eleventh station, I always wondered with frustration why Christ did not come down from the cross and show those mockers His power. He could have, you know. But he held on for me, so I could be forgiven and have good reason to forgive. Though this particular exercise, the stations, is not available in all our denominations, it is always a good idea to take advantage of whatever Holy Week meditations our assemblies offer.

But of all the methods of reflection, God's universal, and best means to *"see Jesus"* – to view His suffering – is the rite of Holy Communion or the Eucharist.

*And as they were eating, Jesus took bread, and blessed it, and broke it, and gave it to the disciples, and said, "Take, eat; this is my body." And He took the cup, and gave thanks, and gave it to them, saying, "Drink all of it; for this is my blood of the New Testament, which is shed for many for the remission of sins."*2

In this sacrament, God sets up an encounter for us with the crucified Christ. We need this because we forgive by looking unto Calvary for the soul we must pardon. By these outward and visible signs of bread and wine, the Holy Spirit awakens us to the inward and invisible grace of God's forgiving love. The apostolic teaching is this: *As often as you eat this bread, and drink this cup, you publically show the Lord's death till He comes.*3

Like Moses' brazen serpent lifted up for snake-bitten Israelites, this ceremony is an antidote for poisons burning our souls. The intimate vision of the afflicted Christ, given to all who trust God, overrides our sense and our senses.

Different Paths Up Calvary

For some, the presented elements are emblems, for others they hold the presence of Christ, and still for others they are the actual body and blood of Jesus in the appearance of bread and wine. Whatever our belief, in our communion with the Uplifted Sacrifice, the Holy Spirit speaks to our hearts of Christ Our Forgiveness. It is God's gift to us *before whose eyes Jesus Christ is displayed, crucified.*4

Do As Occasion Serves; for God Is With You. *1 Samuel 10:7*

The sacrament offers the opportunity and the capacity to forgive. As we approach the altar of cup and bread, Christ presents the blood He shed, not only for us, but also for the sin of our enemies. It is the body broken for any and all who hurt us. We stand on blood-soaked holy ground surrendering all rights to revenge. This blood, poured out for us to see, washes away our sins and the sins committed against us.

152

Sipping the sacramental wine of the punished Christ is acknowledging the atonement for wrongs done to us. Taking the elements, we accept God's sentence upon our enemies: the blood of the ultimate punishment, the broken bread of condemnation – the death of Christ. In communion, we are part of a priesthood[5] offering The Lamb to God for the sins of the world and for the sins of our own particular offenders. To the Heavenly Father, we confess His only begotten Son crucified for sins against us. We pardon others through faith in that blood by which we ourselves are pardoned.[6] In unison with the Eternal Judge we say, *"Father forgive them."*[7]

The hymn writer tells us:
There is a fountain filled with blood
Drawn from Emmanuel's veins
And sinners plunged beneath that flood
Lose all their guilty stains.[8]

We ask God to show us those who damage us "plunged beneath that flood," that we may no longer see the stain of their guilt. There is power in the blood enabling us to forgive.
Would you o'er evil a victory win?
There's wonderful power in the blood.[9]

We receive the sacrament of the body and blood of our savior, leaving all guilt in the "fountain filled with blood;" we walk away from it, knowing it is now fully God's concern.

I am that bread of life. If any man eats of this bread, he shall live forever: and the bread that I will give is my flesh, which I will give for the life of the world. He that eats my flesh, and drinks my blood, as...I live by the Father, so he...shall live by me.[10] The world still finds these words as hard to hear as did the disciples who first heard them. The day Jesus said this, most of them left off following Him saying, "This is hard talk. Who can listen to it?"

The Scandal

As the centuries lumbered forward, philosophers, governments, artists, and comics have mocked and condemned the Eucharistic rite. We should not be surprised, because Jesus told us, *except a man be born again, he cannot understand the sovereign power of God.*[11] None of this makes sense unless we live in Christ, and He lives in us.

*The natural man does not grasp the things of the Spirit of God: for to him they are foolishness: he cannot know them, because they are evaluated spiritually.*12

Feeding The Heart Of Mercy

The Bread of Life nourishes an enemy-loving mercy. Our acts of mercy toward our enemies begin here: embracing the Christ torn for them. Even the blood thirst of our emaciated sense of justice and our hunger for revenge abate at this table. Christ is the broken bread devastating our vindictive hearts as He sops God's judgment.

The Bread Who is Our Forgiveness is more essential to life than our daily fare. Jesus kneads His forgiveness into our daily bread by placing both in the same sentence of the Lord's Prayer. *Give us this day our daily bread, and forgive us our debts as we forgive our debtors.*13 In the Holy Scriptures, *"breaking bread,"* sharing a meal, was a ritual of warm and intimate fellowship. It was during the first Pentecost revival that the infant Church, *breaking bread from house to house, ate their meat with gladness and singleness of heart.*14 If they found their *gladness and singleness of heart* around sharing simple meals, how much more will be our joy and unity if we share the eternal bread of Christ, our forgiveness, from house of God to house of God. As it is so essential to our forgiveness, it is good to celebrate communion more and more rather than less and less.

From our various liturgies

The Gifts of God for the People of God:
take them in remembrance that Christ died for you,
and feed on him in your hearts by faith, with thanksgiving.
This is the Lamb of God
who takes away the sin of the World.
Happy are those who are called to His supper.
The body of our Lord Jesus Christ and His precious blood
strengthen and preserve you unto eternal life.15

The communion service, a miracle in itself, can have an effect that is simply miraculous...

1John 12:21; 2Matthew 26:26-28; 31Corinthians 11:26; 4Galatians 3:1; 5Revelation 5:10; 6Colossians 1:14; 7Luke 23:34; 8There Is a Fountain Filled with Blood by W. Cowper; 9Power in the Blood-LJones; 10John 6:48-57; 11John 3:3; 121Corinthians 2:14; 13Matthew 6:11; 14Acts 2:46; 15Eucharistic Rite: Book of Common Prayer, Order of Mass: Roman Catholic Parish Hymnal, and The Communion: Lutheran Service Book

Chapter Twenty-Eight

Miracles

Then came Peter to him, and said, "Lord, how often shall my brother sin against me, and I forgive him? Till seven times?" Jesus said unto him, "I say not until seven times: but, until seventy times seven. Take heed to yourselves: If your brother trespass against you, rebuke him; and if he repent, forgive him. And if he trespasses against you seven times in a day, and seven times in a day turn again to you, saying, 'I repent'; you shall forgive him."

And the apostles said to the Lord, "Increase our faith."

*And the Lord said, "If you had faith as a grain of mustard seed, you might say unto this sycamore tree, 'Be plucked up by the root, and be planted in the sea'; and it should obey you."'*1

In this passage Jesus equates God's forgiveness in us to a miracle. He, who once invited Peter out for a walk on the water,2 now tells him to take up gardening there. He infers that this walk of forgiveness is like planting an apple orchard in the middle of the Atlantic Ocean. Jesus compares the God-grown act of forgiveness to a miracle. He frames it in a state of affairs that certainly calls for supernatural patience. Seventy times seven comes out to four hundred forty-nine offenses in one day. The brother in question needs to be taken off the street for his own safety. At the very least one should keep a healthy distance from him. But with this humorous exaggeration, Jesus removes all limits from the offer of mercy, intimating that the forgiveness required of us calls for unlimited, miracle working power.

But as a believing Christian, you have already experienced at least one miracle. This unfeasible forgiveness is the outgrowth of the miracle of salvation that lives in you.

The Miracle of Salvation

The first whisper in your heart from the Spirit of Love invited you to live a miracle, to experience the impossible. The moment you first believed, you entered the realm of the miraculous. The disciples heard Jesus declare that the best and worthiest of their people could no more enter the Kingdom of God than a camel could squeeze through the eye of a needle.

They were shocked, and said, "Who then can be saved?"

*But Jesus looked at them, and said, "With men this is impossible; but with God all things are possible."*3

With us salvation is impossible. Christ let's us know that it is a miracle, so that we are not tempted to think that we can do it ourselves.Yet the lowliest believer on the Lord Jesus Christ is forever saved. On this the Apostle is clear, *"If you shall confess with your mouth the Lord Jesus, and shall believe in your heart that God has raised Him from the dead, you shall be saved. For whosoever shall call upon the name of the Lord shall be saved."*4

It is likely that you have called on the name of the Lord, confessing your heart's faith in the resurrected Christ. (If not, by all means, please do so now.) Though *"this is impossible,"* still you are saved. You already stand in the miracle power of God. It appears that you are a miracle of Jesus. This being so, it follows that the day of miracles is still with us. You are saved, and your salvation is a miracle.

The Miracle of Faith

Still, the level of forbearance God calls us to out-strips our natural capacity to comply. It is beyond our own paltry righteousness. He warns of the impossibility of the task in order to bring us running to Him who alone can do this. Seeing the hopelessness of our virtue, we cry with the disciples, *"Increase our faith."*

Jesus had teasingly nicknamed His followers the *"Littlefaiths."*5 Now He tells us that this *"little faith"* we find planted in our hearts can do the impossible. Remember this *faith is not of* *ourselves, it is the gift of God, It is the faith of the Son of God.*6 A wee bit of His faith can *say unto this mountain, "Remove hence to yonder place," and it shall remove; and nothing shall be impossible unto you.*7 Like Peter going to Jesus on the waves, you will walk on mercy; God will hold you up. As you step out of the boat, the water will firm. Move to forgive: the forgiveness will be there. Remember the Israelite's coming to the Jordan to enter Canaan? As the priest's foot touched the water, the river parted, and the nation walked across on dry land.8 If you just put a toe in the water, you will get to where you want to go. The faith of Christ will work for you the miracle of God's forgiveness.

The life of Christ in us is our living faith. Like all living things, it grows. To explain the life of faith, Jesus told a kind of Jack and the Beanstalk tale, about *a grain of mustard seed, which a man took, and cast into his garden; and it grew, and waxed a great tree; and the birds of the air nested in its branches.*9 The mustard seed is about the size of the lowercase "o" in this sentence. My fellow Little-faiths, Christ planted a tiny miraculous kernel in our hearts. As we allow Him to have His way among us, it will become a giant, solid oak of mercy. This miracle working faith is not something we may someday acquire, it is something in us now, which we can learn to exercise.

I'm telling you about these miracles, already active in your life, because you and I are invited to participate in the greatest miracle of all time:

The Miracle of Unity.

Another time Jesus used a mustard seed illustration, *"It is like a grain of mustard seed, which, when it is sown in the earth, is less than all the seeds that be in the earth: But when it is sown, it grows up, and becomes greater than all herbs, and shoots out great branches; so that the fowls of the air may nest under the shadow of it."*10

This time our Lord presents a different version of the parable: the most humble of plants becomes a mighty herb because it reaches out. The mustard plant grows in fields. Thousands of plants extend their branches and support one another as the branches intertwine. Though one plant by itself buckles in a breeze, a flexible field of wind-absorbing herbs may grow as high as eight to fifteen feet. Some report plants climbing as high as thirty feet in this supportive entanglement.

This miraculous seed of faith and love is present in all hearts confessing the Lord Jesus. It is in you, and it is in me. Like the fields of mustard, we *may be knit together in love.*[11]

Our unity is His next miracle, made possible by His forgiveness and forbearance planted in our hearts...

1Matthew18:21-22 & Luke17:5,6; 2Matthew 14:29; 3Matthew19:26; 4Romans 10:9,13; 5Luke 12:28; 6Ephesians 2:10; Galatians 2:20; 7Matthew 17:20; 8Joshua 3:13; 9Luke 13:19; 10Mark 4:31-33; 11Colossians 2:2`

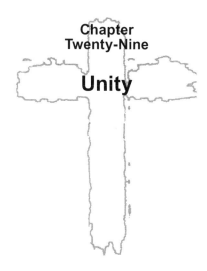

Chapter
Twenty-Nine

Unity

Jessie had a chronic case of severe eczema. During flare-ups, the tips of his fingers cracked and bled, keeping him from the activity he loved: playing the guitar. He promised the Lord that if healed, he would play only worship Music. He believed the condition was punishment for the years he played what some call, "the devil's music:" the blues.

I explained, "I don't believe that, Jesse. God doesn't make His children sick. And you know what: the devil may use music, but none of it is his... especially not the blues."

We are here in this spiritual war zone, and we suffer from the fall of the species. Until it all shakes out, God will use even the illness we endure to create our good, but the punishment for our sin is placed upon Christ crucified, not upon us. We are completely and perfectly forgiven. Many believers think they are not healed because they are not worthy to be healed. Remember, remember, and always remember: Christ is our worthiness. And how worthy is the Lamb? As the *angels and the ten thousand times ten thousand, and thousands of thousands round about the throne* in heaven cry out; *"Worthy is the Lamb that was slain to receive power, and riches, and wisdom, and strength, and honor,*

163

and glory, and blessing."₁ Healing fits in the categories of blessing, power, riches, and strength. Christ The Lamb, sacrificed for our sin, qualifies you and me worthy of healing. He is our Qualification. That's how complete His forgiveness is.

The Unhealed

I heard a young paraplegic woman tell the heartbreaking story of a healing meeting. The ushers kept all the folks who were in wheel chairs out of sight, far away from the stage where the evangelist laid hands on the sick and lame. The choir droned,

"Savior, Savior, hear my humble cry;
While on others thou art calling do not pass me by."₂

But it seemed that the Savior was passing them by. At the end of the meeting, with the weight of shame crushing their souls, the wheel-chaired were silently escorted out the back door of the arena. Humiliation flooded their minds with questions, "What is wrong with me? Everyone will know I am a doubter. Why is my faith so small?"

The Ambush Of Doubt

On the other side of the story, the minister lives in a dull panic. He or she bears the weight of being "God's man/woman of the hour; full of faith and power." It cultivates fertile ground for hypocrisy.

Jill suffered from debilitating back pain. Out in public, her husband pushed her wheel chair. She could walk, but it was just more convenient to use the chair. Besides, the fabric of the wheel chair was easier on her back. At staircases, she got out of the chair while Tony carried it up. Then she sat back down and off they rolled, laughing about the puzzled looks on the faces of bystanders. When Brother Somebody, who had the big healing ministry, was in town, they were at the coliseum early. Once on stage, Rev. Somebody leaned over and asked, so that only Jill could hear, "What is the problem, Sister?"

"It's my back," said Jill, "I'm in almost constant pain. I can walk. I don't need this wheel chair. Do you want me to stand up?"

"No, no," replied the minister, "That won't be necessary." Then, into the microphone he shouted for all to hear, "Sister, in the name of Jesus Christ, get out of that wheel chair, and walk."

Jill was stunned. She stood up and walked off the stage to the cheers of the audience. Deeply hurt, she left her church, and began to look into the occult.

Did the preacher lack the faith to exercise the gift of healing? Did the paraplegic woman lack the faith to see God's miracle working power? The short answer is, "Yes, every one lacks that faith."

The Family Heritage

Miracle working faith is not the gift of the individual member of the body of Christ; it is of the whole body. It is the faith of the spiritual community. At times it shows up in isolated cases, but as we all know, it is rare. It is exceptional. A consistent manifestation of this faith requires unity in the family of Jesus Christ. No single person controls it. It is not a gift possessed by the super spiritual in our midst. An old cowboy preacher once told me, "God has no big shots, just a bunch of little shots that keep shootin'." Though expressed through one member of the body of Christ, it is borne by the whole. It is not the individual who is healed so much as it is the Church who is healed.

Here is how Paul says it works, *"In Jesus Christ no religious practice or non-practice wields power, but only the faith, which works through love."*3

The thing that makes faith work is the love of God shared between us. Love propels faith. Christ's love in us moves His faith given to us. If there is no **us,** there is no power-exerting faith. This Love does not exist in a vacuum, standing alone, embracing the no one in the nothingness around it. Love is not the isolated saint secluded in a forest hermitage, or hiding in a sanctuary. The solitude of nature may be a wonderful cathedral, but it is not a church. Because love happens face to face, Paul encourages, *"Let us consider one another and contend for love's beautiful business, and not abandon the gathering of ourselves together."*4

Love is the noisy, crowded life of the family of God. We are one in Christ. Though individually saved, the individual is saved into the community of faith. The life of Christ is not aloof and solitary. God's compassion breathes and grows in our fellowship. Unforgiveness breaks that fellowship. Any break in that fellowship

165

weakens the faith necessary to seat the miracle working power of God in the front pew.

The Greatest of These is Love 1Corinthians 13:13

The first miracle needed in the Church is an about-face from contention *unto the genuine, unpretentious love of the brethren.*5 In describing this love Paul declares that it *bears all things, believes all things, hopes all things, and endures all things.*6 The love of God in us does all the believing, hoping, and putting up with others; the forbearing and forgiving by faith. The Love, who resides in our spirits, believes and animates our faith. We know faith is alive because it moves. A faith without action is a faith without love, not the faith of the Son of God.7 The faith to see miracles is a natural characteristic of Love. Paul again describes love, saying, *"The fruit of this Spirit is love: joy, peace, longsuffering, gentleness, goodness, faith, meekness, temperance: against such there is no law."*8 Faith, and all the rest in the description, is a vital attribute of that Love who is God in us.

We and Us

The apostle teaches that God, in the gathering, *is able to do exceeding abundantly above all that we ask or think, according to the power that works in us.*9 It is not written, "the power that works in me," or " the power that works in you," but the apostle says, *"us".*

Jesus also uses the word *"us"* in the Lord's Prayer: *"Forgive us our debts."*10 Because we are one in Christ, I can forgive for you and you for me. We can join in forgiving. We can stand and forgive for the wounded among us who struggle with deep pain. Because we are one body, the forgiveness will find the affected member and bring peace. Does this sound unlikely? Try it first, church of God; then judge.

The Lord our righteousness, love, redemption, peace, and power promised to be present, *"when two or three of you are gathered in My name."*11 He said *"two or three,"* because the tender shoots of love stand the best chance in small numbers. In the intimacy of the small group, we confess our hurts and struggles, and we can pray out forgiveness with any one member.

It is when we are rooted and grounded in love, that we are able to know the love of Christ, which surpasses the knowledge of any one person. But together we can comprehend the breadth, and length, and depth, and height of it. As a people, we can be filled with all the fullness of God. That is when He will receive glory in the church by Christ Jesus. That is when the world will shake with the power of God's love. Notice the plurality of this passage. *That Christ may dwell in* **your** *hearts by faith; that* **you**, (as in "You all") *being rooted and grounded in love, May be able to comprehend with* **all saints** *what is the breadth, and length, and depth, and height; And to know the love of Christ, which passes knowledge, that you might be filled with all the fullness of God. Now unto Him that is able to do exceeding abundantly above all that* **we** *ask or think, according to the power that works in* **us**, *unto Him be glory in* **the church** *by Christ Jesus throughout all ages, world without end. Amen.*12

Reason to Behave

Given that the miracle working power of God thrives in the love of His people, we can see why Paul goes on to tell us to *behave with all lowliness and meekness, with patience, forbearing one another in love; endeavoring to keep the unity of the Spirit in the bond of peace.*13 To protect the healing unity, we endeavor to let Christ live out the forgiveness of God in us. *We labor to enter into that rest*14 in Him. For the sake of those who need the power of God to move on their behalf, we approach each other in the mood of Spirit-imbued tolerance.

The Bible describes us as the Body of Christ. *Christ Himself is the head from whom the whole body – affectionately fit and knit together by the working of every single fiber, as each part does its part – increases and builds itself up in love.*15 The forgiveness that God has put in our hearts holds us together despite our weaknesses. Our togetherness will bring His health and wholeness into our world. We need what God has hidden in each one of our hearts if this body is to be strong, healthy, and whole. Just as every part of a body needs every other part so we need each other.

*And whether one member suffer, all the members suffer with it; or one member be honored, all the members rejoice with it.*16 If I think my little resentment won't matter to the whole, I deceive myself and injure all. We are members one of another; the life I live affects you, and your life affects me. When I separate from the body, it is like a tear that weakens the whole. No one of us is indispensable in the work God wants to do. I need you; you need me; we all need each other. There is no such thing as a nonessential member.

Healed

Jesus once mentioned the proverb, *"physician heal yourself".*[17] As we look at our condition today, church of God, we may well do with that advice. We, the church of Christ, often exhibit dysfunction, disability, and immaturity. But if we give ourselves to *forbearing one another, and forgiving one another... even as Christ forgave us,*[18] (presenting His blood to the justice of God,) then we will finally start to *grow up. Till we all come in the unity of the faith...to a mature person,...to the measure of the stature of the fullness of Christ.*[19] Jesus is the *"mature person"* spoken of here. The *"mature person"* we come to is the Christ. Together, we grow up into Him. It is our Lord Jesus Christ who works the miracles, and heals the sick. We all know this. If we unite in His Love, Christ the Miracle Worker will stand full stature in our midst, healing the weak, mending the broken hearted, and raising the dead. Let all the Mustard-Seed-Little-Faiths unite in His love so that the tree of life will stretch branches over our field.

The Main Attraction

The world will not be drawn to Christ by signs and wonders, but by the miracle of a loving united people. It has always been so. In the mid nineteen-sixties, tens of thousands flocked to California because they believed a loving community existed there. Of course, it was but an illusion of selfish hedonism that eventually wrought death and disease around the world. But the thought of a group of loving people touched a chord in millions of souls, and drew them to the west coast.

We hold forth no fantasy. In very truth, the God who is love lives in our midst. Unbelievers shall be drawn to Him in faith, as we believers move by Him in love for one another.

Jesus assures us, *"By this shall all men know that you are My disciples, if you have love one to another."*[20] Knowing that we are His disciples, the world will come looking for Him, for He is *The Desire of the Nations.*[21] As Simon told Him, *"All men seek for thee.*"22 The people of the world will see that Jesus is present when the Forgiving Love of God is so strong with us that sin, sickness, and death flee our gatherings. As He said,

"And I,
if I be lifted up from the earth,
*will draw all men unto me."*23

We shall then forgive.

1Revelation 5:12; 2F Crosby; 3Galatians 5:6; 4Hebrews 10:24-25; 51Peter 1:22; 61Corinthians 13:7; 7Galatians2:20; 8Galatians5:22-23; 9Ephesians3:20; 10Matthew6:12; 11Matthew18:20; 12Ephesians17-21; 13Ephesians4:3; 14Hebrews4:11;15Ephesians4:16; 161Corinthians12:26; 17Luke4:23; 18Colossians3:13;19Ephesians4:13; 20John 13:35; 21Haggai 2:7; 22Mark 1:37; 23John 12:32

Made in the USA
San Bernardino, CA
06 November 2014